teaching children to swim

Acknowledgments

The author and publisher would like to thank the parents of
the children whose photographs were taken for use in this book.
The children concerned are:
Kathleen Higgins, Peter and Sandra Cole, John Collins,
Tracy Clements, Sabra Platt, Darren Anthony,
Michael Stringfellow, Martin Tromp, Juliette Vidilini.
Photography was by Alvin Lawson.
Cover: Martin Brennan

Published by Paul Hamlyn Pty Ltd,
176 South Creek Road, Dee Why West,
New South Wales, 2099
© Copyright: Paul Hamlyn Pty Ltd, 1971
First published 1971
Reprinted 1972
Printed by Lee Fung, Hong Kong
ISBN 0 600 07054 9
Design: Hugh McLeod

teaching children to swim

eva bory

HG
paul hamlyn
sydney · london
new york · toronto

Preface-
Forbes Carlile

The quicker this book is in print the happier my wife, Ursula, and I will be because we want to make it required study for all teachers and coaches in our various pools in Sydney and Melbourne. We want to see all the parents of our younger pupils with their personal copy.

Of all the elementary swimming instruction books we have read, this is the most unique and the most essentially practical.

So it should be. Eva, our Head Teacher at Ryde for some years and then at her own swimming school at Toongabbie, has nearly twenty-two years' swimming experience (of which twelve were of teaching), great enthusiasm, and a keen analytical mind to develop an approach to swimming that really works. As a Hungarian Olympic swimmer she knows swimming from A to Z. Add to this that priceless ingredient of enthusiasm and the result is something which should surely be a standard work to be read by all those who teach swimming.

This is no 'scissors and paste' job, filled with half-baked ideas of others. This book is an *original* piece of work made all the more interesting because Eva, with her own young daughter, had the opportunity to practise what she preached, and to learn.

This book will be of great value to the sport of swimming in Australia.

Eva Bory is to be congratulated. Her rare sense of humour comes bubbling through in her newly acquired language. She writes as she thinks and speaks. The result is the best book yet on beginning swimming, for Eva Bory is that rare person, a great swimmer and a natural-born teacher.

If you have children, or you are in the position to help any children in their swimming, then this book is worth many times the price.

Forbes Carlile, M.Sc.,
Former Australian
Olympic Coach,
Ryde, N.S.W.

Contents

Swimming and the teaching of it~ Some general thoughts and advice.   11

games and preparation in the bathroom 15, washing hair 16, how young can a baby swim? 16, home pools 20, what swim costume to wear 25, swimming aids 26, asthma and swimming 29, disabled children 30, you can teach your child to swim 30

Teaching the three to five year olds.   38

how many in a class? 41, teaching the easy way 42, words to use 45, kicking board use 51, dog paddling 56, blowing bubbles 60, learning to float 64, opening eyes under water 67, going stale 71, kicking on the back 74, jump and dive 74

Five to ten year olds~ advanced swimming.   86

arm movement in freestyle 90, breathing 90, faults—(too much kicking 95, not enough kicking 95, holding breath 96, stopping 97, left-arm drag 98, head out of water 98, can't get rid of air 100, lack of stamina 101, ugly style 101), swim drill, land drill 104, deep water 104

Teaching backstroke, butterfly, breaststroke.   110

on competitive swimming 110, butterfly stroke 114, butterfly breathing 119, dolphin kick 120, backstroke 123, breaststroke 125, freestyle 130, bi-lateral breathing 134, four-stroke breathing 137

Swimming and the teaching of it~
Some general thoughts and advice.

Swimming is the only sport in which the whole family can participate together. Just think—your girls are doing physical culture, ballet, music, the boys are off to soccer, football, father is playing golf, mother is playing the glorified role of being the chauffeur to everybody—the family rarely has an outing together, except to the beach.

Parents who can't swim and are afraid of water must be careful not to transfer their fear to the children. If for some reason, a child has a fear of water, be patient in trying to overcome it.

The big problem of the non-swimming parent is 'what do I do when my child falls in? I can't go in and save him.' It is for these parents that this book is written. If your child is confident, he can be independent and save himself.

The best way of preparing a child to swim in a swimming pool is to start a thorough preparation in the bathroom.

Newborn babies are not afraid of water. Their fear comes from new experiences or can be sensed from their mother's attitude towards water and swimming. Generally, a child who has never seen a dog will be quite unconcerned, walk up to it, pat it, but if his mother says 'Don't touch it, it will bite you', the child will become frightened or at least wary.

All the mothers I have known through the years, except the very rare few, were terrified of giving their newborn baby the first bath at home.

Those mothers who handle their baby inexpertly, hesitantly, affect the child adversely. If a mother knows what she is supposed to do and handles the child confidently, the child will benefit from that and be confident, too. But, of course, no new mother is very expert to begin with.

In hospital, waiting to go home after having my first baby, I was scared of many things but one thing I was really looking forward to was giving my baby her first bath.

I did everything as shown to me at the hospital, then when I got her out of the water and dried her, just from curiosity, I started to pull and pinch her little arms and legs and to my amazement I discovered that they were very well made and they didn't fall off. She was tiny all right, but at the same time she was a little human being.

I was determined to get this baby of mine swimming at a very early age. Up to that time I had only had experience in teaching with children two years and onwards, since no sane mother would take a three-weeks-old baby to a swimming lesson. Or would she?

At the baby clinic, the nurses advised me to get into the routine of bathing the baby before the 10 o'clock meal. I did this for about a week and then I had to do some serious thinking. The baby was yelling and screaming from the minute I undressed her to get her ready for her bath and the planned playtime in the bath was nothing but a screaming session.

I supposed that she was crying so much because she was very, very hungry. So, I changed tactics and from then on I used to feed her at 10 o'clock, let her rest for about 10 to 15 minutes while I got the bath ready, and then we started on our daily fun session. It was a tremendous change, her belly was full, she was happy in the water and completely relaxed, and, boy, did she sleep after her bath!

In three weeks she was floating on her back, with a little support under her head. I made sure that she was in and under the water as much as possible. Lying on her back, her ears were completely submerged and when I was holding her I would gently splash some water on her face. Neighbours and friends who came to see me at bathtime were horrified.

'What are you doing to her? You're killing her!'

'Don't worry, I know what I'm doing.'

I must add, none of their children were swimming at eighteen months.

Baby is happy and relaxed in the bath. Note how the water level comes past the ears.

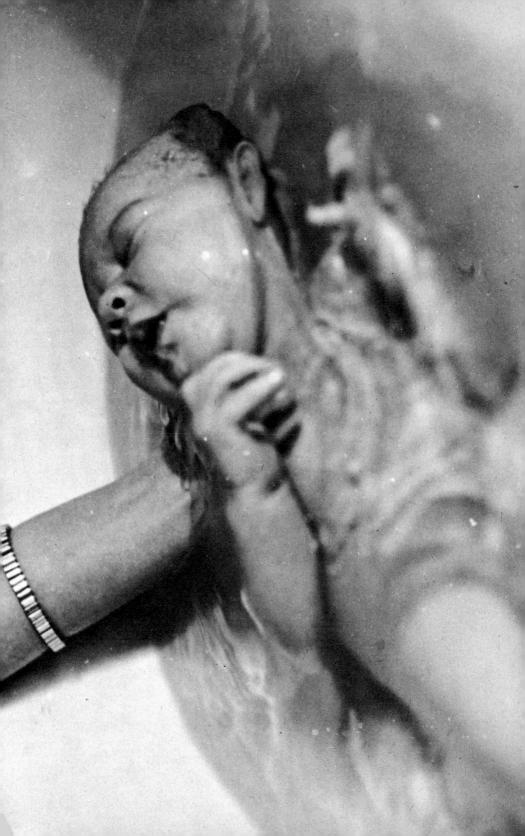

GAMES AND PREPARATION IN THE BATHROOM

As soon as possible, transfer your baby from his usual bath to the family bathtub. Fill the bath to about 3 inches deep so that when baby lies flat on his back the water just comes past his ears. Gently splash some water over his face so he can get used to being wet all over. Take a chair into the bathroom and if the phone rings don't answer it, if somebody is at the door don't take any notice. Once babies master the art of sitting up, they seldom like to lie down again. Once he sits up, transfer him to the shower.

The water pressure of the shower shouldn't be too strong. Make sure he has plenty of toys to play with, especially empty plastic bottles. He can fill them up with water, and can pour the water out, and so on.

As a baby grows he does more adventurous things. Tell him to kick his legs—first move his legs to show how it's done. Mother can put her face in the water and show how to blow bubbles, but remember always come up smiling. Don't ever show panic if your kiddie suddenly slips and disappears under the water. Lift him out quickly, efficiently, put a big smile on your face (even if your heart beats two hundred times a minute), and say, 'That was great! Will you show that to mummy again?' This way the child will assume that going under the water is fun and it's not something to be afraid of.

When your baby is little he can only lie on his back. Put your hands under his head to support him and gently move him backwards and forwards in the bath. From about eight months onwards he can be rolled onto his tummy.

Alternate between having a shower and a bath and try not to make bathtime a rushed affair. Try to organise housework so you can spend a comfortable twenty minutes or more in the bathroom. When letting the water out of the bath, don't have the baby there with you. Very often it makes a very loud noise which can frighten a baby. Dr Spock advises the same.

It's a good idea to have children wear a proper swimming cap in the bath. Having a cap on protects the hair and theoretically it should stay dry. If you have a water bug as your baby and he wants to do all sorts of tricks in the bathtub

Do I look funny to you too?

you would often be tempted to say, 'Be careful, don't get your hair wet,' which, of course, is the main source of fun. Even on cold, wintery nights, children can frolic in the bath, provided they are wearing a cap.

WASHING HAIR
In nine out of ten families washing hair is a dreaded occasion. Children yell, scream and carry on. These are the children who are not used to having their faces and ears completely wet and find it most uncomfortable to go through the hair-washing and rinsing process.

If children are accustomed to being wet all over it doesn't worry them. Always use *baby shampoo,* which doesn't sting the eyes. Don't use soap or your own brand of shampoo just because it happens to be handy. The easiest way to wash hair is in the bath, in a sitting position, and for rinsing simply make them lie down. If children are made to get used to the shower early enough, washing hair under the shower should cause no problem. Girls can take their dolls in the shower. Say, 'You wash dolly's hair and I'll wash yours.'

For rinsing, say, 'Stand right under the shower and rinse dolly's hair.'

Another good game is to make all sorts of funny shapes with the lather, especially if they can see themselves in a mirror. Washing hair can be fun, if you make the effort.

HOW YOUNG CAN A BABY SWIM?
People often ask me how young can a baby swim? How old should he be when he starts having lessons?

There is a lot of confusing information. I'm sure we have all heard the story of how in New Guinea the natives throw their children into rivers and they swim out like ducks. That could be true, but nobody has specified how *old* these children were.

We see from time to time in newspapers and magazines, photos of babies—and I mean babies—two or three months old, floating. Studying these photos, you can see that the head is never out of the water, it is always face down, and you can see

16

This baby is 4 months old and she is totally absorbed with the cameraman under the water.

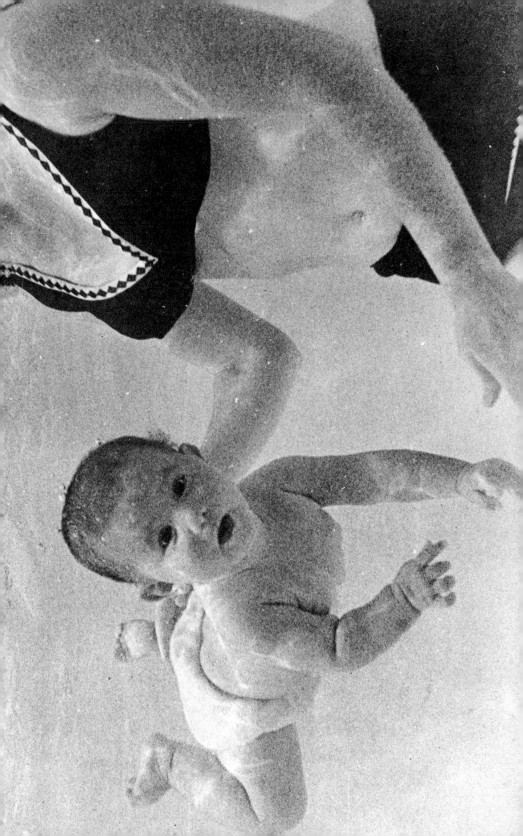

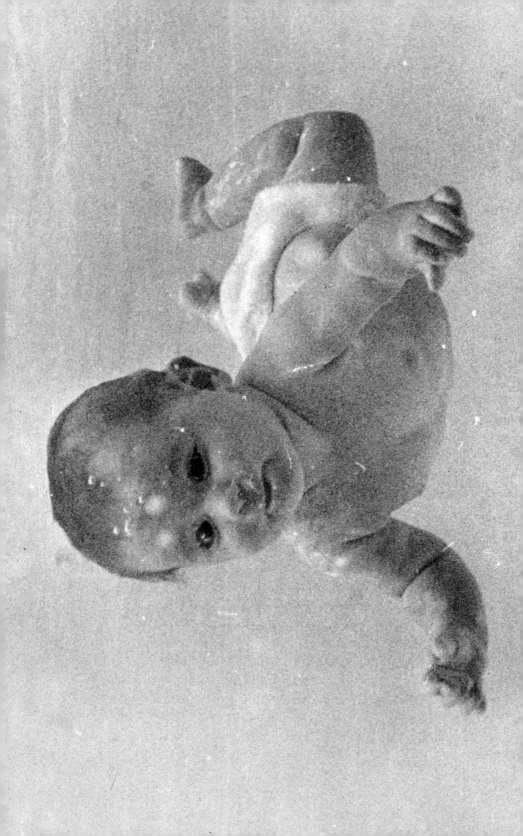

the shadow of a person standing very close by. Children automatically hold their breath under the water, so when placed in the water, they naturally float on top. But, unfortunately, when they are very young they are not able to lift their heads above the water to take a breath; the instructor or the parent has to stand close by to lift them out when they run out of breath.

Some people might call this 'swimming', but, in my opinion, swimming is when a person or a child can swim a given distance in deep water confidently, breathing regularly, *not* holding their breath.

There is a lot to be said for getting young babies accustomed to floating. When there are so many private swimming pools around it can be a matter of life and death. If there is sufficient training beforehand, it is possible that a baby can fall off the edge of the pool, make a U-turn and hold onto the edge again.

There *are* swimming instructors who specialise in teaching young babies. It's all very well to get an expert, qualified instructor to come to your home to give a three-minute lesson, three to five times a week, for as long as a year, but, at fees up to $5.00 a lesson, few can afford it.

This little book on preparation and teaching swimming will, I hope, fill the present gap of available books on the subject.

In our own swimming school we start teaching children from two years onwards, giving them one or two half-hour lessons a week. Admittedly, it would be much better for the children concerned to have a daily dip of about five minutes, but many obstacles, travelling long distances, etc., preclude this.

I think all children should be taught correctly by qualified instructors, but before any actual lessons mothers can help by going through a preparation procedure with the child. When the child is ready, then he can be brought along to be taught the correct breathing, and the arm and leg action.

In my 12 years of teaching experience I have only seen two children who were free swimmers before the age of two. With certain swimming aids, an eight-month-old could swim, if the training started early enough.

This little one is perfectly happy under the water but doesn't have the strength to come up for air on her own.

When a child begins at a swimming school, about five lessons, at least, are wasted on the teacher and child getting to know each other. So mothers ought to do all they can in proper preparation, especially in making sure the child has no fear of the water.

This, remember, can only be achieved by refusing to give in to your own fears. A parent's fear is very easily transferred to the child, if the parent is not careful.

HOME POOLS

In every backyard, nowadays, there is usually some form of a swimming pool. It varies from a plastic 18 inch pool to a luxurious, sunken, deep, tiled pool. If you have a backyard pool of any type I feel it is very important that children should be swimming on their own by the time they are three years old. If you don't own a boat or a swimming pool or have some rich friends who do, you can leave the learning-to-swim till they are five or six.

If you are just thinking of building a new pool, my advice is to provide a shallow end for the children. Even if the occupants of the house are people with no children, I would still advise providing a small area which is not deep and can be used for non-swimmers and, of course, for young children.

If space permits, the most practical pool to build, in my opinion, is a T-shaped pool. One end of the 'T' should be very shallow, from 18 inches to 2 feet. The other end of the 'T' for diving should be 8 feet deep, while the long end of the 'T' would be used for swimming and would be about 4 feet deep all through.

The next best thing would be an L-shaped pool. If there is no room for spreading out sideways, you should build fairly wide steps which can serve the purpose of a wading area.

I'm very much against building odd shaped pools, the most popular being the kidney shape. They look very pretty and picturesque, but they are completely useless. The only way you can swim in a kidney-shaped pool is around and around, like a goldfish.

All swimming pools should have a cover, preferably wire-

mesh, to protect children from falling in. A wire-mesh cover can save on maintenance, too.

When you consider building a pool, try to think ahead and make provision for pipes to be laid for eventually heating the pool. Australia is supposed to be 'sunny Australia', but in fact, if you have an outdoor pool, the only comfortable use you can get out of it would be from November till middle of March, if you're lucky. Children will go into the water for playing in all sorts of freezing, miserable conditions, but we parents have to think of our own comfort and pleasures. Initial cost of a heater is high but the actual running cost is surprisingly low. There are gas heaters, electric heaters, fuel heaters, so shop around.

WHAT TYPE OF SWIMMING COSTUMES TO WEAR

When taking your baby into the swimming pool for the daily dip, the best thing for the baby to wear is nothing. But this is not always practicable. To have a nappy on is too bulky, so little bikini-type pants are the best. If the baby is very small, small sizes are not usually available, so I'm afraid mum has to sew one.

For little girls the same type of bikini bottom is advisable and I'm personally very much against having those horrid two-piece costumes on little girls. The top part usually slips up around their necks, and the shoulder straps are always falling down.

You should pay close attention to the type of swimming costume sour children wear because a lot of bad habits in swimming can be caused by the wrong type of costume. With some children I have known, I have had to battle to get their arms properly out of the water. Having constantly to pull their fallen shoulder straps back, they had got used to holding one arm under the water, all the time.

For those mothers who will be going into the pool teaching their young ones, I also strongly recommend the one-piece type of costume. Children have a tendency of grabbing and pulling at shoulder straps.

Swimming children can rarely afford the luxury of having long hair. For boys, the hair must not come down past their

25

If there is sufficient training beforehand, it is possible that a baby can fall off the edge of the pool, make a U-turn and hold on to the edge again.

eyebrows. For girls, the same applies, and if they have shoulder-length hair, I prefer it to be tied up, either in a ponytail or two pigtails, so that when they come up for air, the hair doesn't interfere with their breathing. Bobby-pins are a nuisance. They don't stay in place and all swimming pool owners hate the sight of them. Many types of pool bottoms are marked by bobby-pins. If the pool is tiled, it is still an extra nuisance picking them up, because the vacuum cleaner does not suck them up and you have to either dive in and fish them out with your hands or do it with a magnet. But whichever way it's done, bobby-pins are a curse!

SWIMMING AIDS

There are many types of swimming aids available in Australia. All of them have their useful purposes . . . **WARNING** A non-swimmer should not rely on a swimming aid unless he is familiar with water.

A lot of people are reluctant to use them on their children thinking they get too dependent on them. Fortunately, this is not so. When children feel confident to do things they discard them, just as they discard milk bottles, dummies, etc. I'm going to list the swimming aids available and will deal with them separately, discussing their usefulness in a later chapter.

Kicking-board

There are many varieties and shapes available—polyfoam, smooth plastic, wood, fibreglass. The best and cheapest would be a polyfoam. Try to get the smallest and thinnest. Children can hold on to it much easier.

Floats

I call them 'magic eggs', also known as bubbles, eggs, pixie-floats. There are a few on the market which you can inflate and they are covered with a material. I like to use the 'magic egg' type, made of polyfoam. It lasts the longest, but the straps will eventually rot in the chlorinated water. Always double check the buckle. When you put an egg on don't tie it too tight around the tummy; leave about a two-finger space between the strap and the flesh. The water lifts the egg up and if the strap is tied too tightly it will cut into the tummy and be most uncomfort-

26

Hold the baby in front of you so that you can see the face all the time.

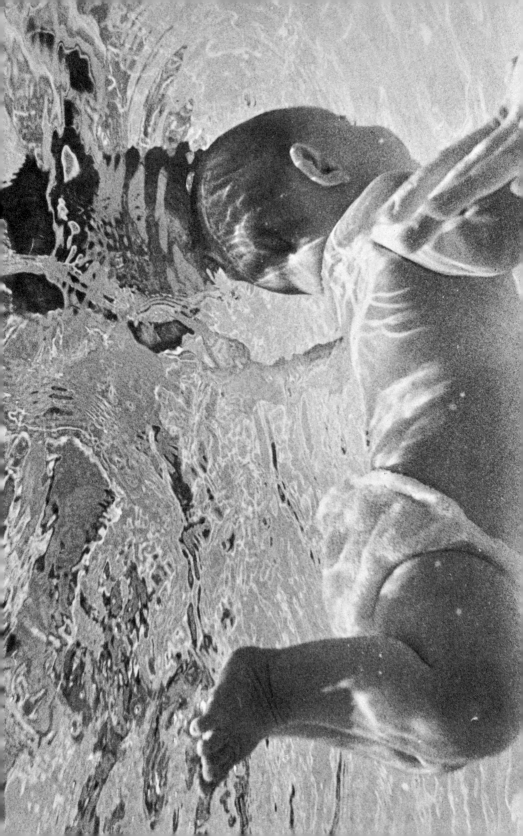

able. When putting the buckle on, as a safety measure, I always tie a tight knot around it to have it 'child-proofed'.

Floaties

These are arm bands which could be useful for the very young but I personally don't like to use them as a teaching aid because they restrict arm movement.

Flippers

Flippers can be very useful, children love them but they are the only swimming aid which can be habit forming and the only one which they don't want to get rid of.

In early learning stages flippers can be very useful, but make sure that on every occasion they wear them there is an equal amount of time swimming without them. If you find that your child gets too dependent on them, lose one and if it's necessary, lose the other as well.

When I'm dealing with the five-to-ten age group, I will explain in detail the advantages and disadvantages of the flipper kick.

Goggles and snorkels

Goggles are very dangerous in swimming pools. They are fun at the beach. When you get a pair of goggles for your child, be on the lookout for they will want to duck under the water all the time.

ASTHMA AND SWIMMING

By now it's a well-known fact that asthma sufferers get great relief when they take up swimming. More and more doctors are realising this and send children for swimming tuition.

Swimming doesn't cure asthma, but in many cases it certainly helps. A lot depends at what age children get asthma. The younger they are, the more chance they have of recovering from it.

Why is swimming so helpful? It expands the lungs, it teaches regular rhythmic breathing: instead of doing boring breathing exercises, the children have fun while they swim, and they don't realise that while they are having fun it is helping them to get better. But just blowing bubbles into the water

29

Let the baby go once so he will float face down. Once floating, don't step back.

doesn't help much; breathing must be synchronised with regular, correct swimming strokes. This is where heated swimming pools are essential because children, and adults, can practise right through the year.

If you have a two-year-old child who suffers from asthma, it could be one year (because of his undeveloped physical co-ordination) before the swimming is beneficial. Remember, to teach an asthmatic child to swim usually takes longer than it would another child; because of the breathing disability they have a justified fear of holding their faces under the water. It takes time and patience and an understanding instructor.

HANDICAPPED AND DISABLED CHILDREN

If a handicapped or disabled child learns to swim, it not only helps him physically but it gives a tremendous boost to his ego. I can't think of any other sport in which, say, somebody with one leg, could compete on equal terms with other people.

In Hungary, there was a very famous long-distance swimmer who had lost one leg and he was National Champion for many years. In swimming, the kicking of the legs is not all that important, it rather serves as a balance to the arms, so if someone is without a leg, they can kick with one leg only. Usually they develop very strong muscles on their upper bodies and that often compensates for the lack of leg movement.

Slow learners at school could become excellent pupils after they have mastered the art of swimming. I have known a few children who had bad stutters. After they came to me they improved so much that they did not need speech therapy any more.

YOU CAN TEACH YOUR CHILD TO SWIM

As we've said, the best place to start is in the bathroom. If the child is completely familiar with the water, is used to having his ears, eyes, nose, mouth in the water, then the first visit to the swimming pool shouldn't cause any problem.

Children are ready to be taken out of doors at the age of two or three months provided the weather is warm, the water is over 76° and you keep the 'lesson' short. If the baby can't walk yet, it is best that the water be no deeper than waist deep,

Perfect body position.

about 3 feet 6 inches.

You hold the baby under the arms in front of you so that you can see his face all the time. This is a golden rule which should be observed *all* the time. Try not to put suntan lotion on the baby, as he will be too slippery to handle safely. If he has tender skin, rather put on a singlet and leave the lotion until he is out of the water.

Slowly start moving backwards so the child swims forward. Keep repeating, 'Kick, kick, kick'. Children at this age have a natural tendency to move their legs: it could be a frog-kick, it could be a bent-knee kick, it could be anything. Don't correct the natural kick. Try not to talk about anything else, just say, 'Kick, kick, kick!' Don't say, 'Would you please mind moving your legs for mummy?'

Just say, 'Kick, kick, kick!'

Each day when you put the baby into the water, let the baby go under *once,* so he will float face down. When you do that, watch and make sure that he takes a breath in. Once he is floating, don't step back. Hold your arms out ready to pick him up, but give him sufficient time—five to ten seconds—to float. After each performance, pick him up and say, 'That was very clever, darling'. Even if everything turned out right don't let go of the child more than *once* each session in the first couple of weeks. If the child comes up screaming or has drunk some water, don't worry. Each day repeat the floating procedure.

Little children will also automatically open their eyes under the water. They can see your legs and swimming costume and are thus assured that you are still there. If the child is not floating on top of the water but sinks down like a rock, the fault is yours. He should be in a horizontal position before you let him go and not have his feet hanging down. I have known some two-year-olds, when swimming, take a breath, then completely disappear to the bottom of the pool. They then work themselves up to the top of the water for a breath and down they go again. For unsuspecting onlookers it could be a frightening sight, but these children are confident in the water and no harm will come to them. At the very early stage style and beauty don't come into it, only confidence, familiarity

33

The child is relaxed and the teacher supports him under the head.

with the water, and safety.

Once the basic face-down floating has been accomplished, you should combine it with movement through the water. You do this by slowly starting to move backwards. Lift the child up by the shoulders, making sure that the head is clearly above the water. Let him take a breath and gently ease him back into the water. Do it two or three times on each occasion but increase the distance day by day. A child should float face down for no longer than five seconds before being lifted up to breathe.

Some children will hold onto the air and when their head is up they will let the air out, take a breath, and duck down again. Children from two months to two years are too little to understand any verbal instruction, so the mother or teacher has to follow the child's natural breathing pattern. When the floating is pretty good and the child is kicking continuously, you can hold one shoulder only and put the other hand under the child's chin to help him up for air.

The arms will also move under the water either in a dog-paddling way or something which resembles breaststroke arm movement. Encourage the children to move their arms under the water and not over, because if they bring their arms out of the water they are bound to make a big splash which interferes with their breathing.

I don't like to use any swimming aids on the very, very young. The 'magic egg' is too bulky for their little bodies and it upsets their flotation face down. I normally use the 'magic egg' on children over two years of age.

Floating on the back

Stand behind the child and hold the back of his head with the palm of your hand, fingers stretched out, the index finger being straight under the neck, giving a firm support. With your left hand gently push the chin backwards, pull the tummy up, straighten the legs out, push the shoulders down. The right hand stays under the head all the time, whilst the left hand will correct the body position.

Start slowly moving backwards, bend over the child's face, especially if there is a strong sun, to shield his eyes with your shadow. Don't encourage kicking, rather have the arms moving under the water like a goldfish's fins. If he kicks, he will tend to overkick and that unbalances the body position.

When the child is relaxed, he will lie very still in a completely horizontal position, then you can take your right hand away; just let it stay a few inches under the water beneath his head. When you do this tap one finger on the child's head, to let him know that you are there ready to catch him if he falls. But he will feel that the water is holding him up without any support from you. Later on you can move your hands further down but keep close by, ready to lift. Don't be too casual; you will need to be prepared to lift him for some time after.

Remember when you are teaching a child to dog-paddle, *always* stay in front of him. When teaching backstroke, *always* stay behind his head. If the going is good you can turn him gently from kicking on his back to dog-paddling and then back again. Children between two and three years old find this terrific fun. If such young children can dog-paddle and kick on their backs, they have done very well.

Teaching the correct swimming stroke (lifting arms out of the water, correct, regular, controlled breathing) comes later.

Jumping and diving

Jumping in the water is as important as learning to swim.

A child has to have the experience of what it feels like to go down to the bottom of the pool and then come up again. After all, the dreaded accidents happen by getting thrown in, pushed in or falling into the water.

Babies should be set up on the edge of the pool. Mother should stand back in the water, arms outstretched so that the tips of her fingers just touch the baby's hands. Gently pull the baby in. When doing this, say, 'Ready . . . go!', so that after a while the baby gets accustomed to taking a breath at 'ready' because he will know that at 'go' he will hit the water.

Later on, mother should stand a few feet further back but still with her arms out ready to catch. Between the age of two and three years they can stand up on the edge of the pool and jump from there. More about jumping and diving when I deal with the three-to-five-year-olds.

36, 37 *Mummy, are you ready?*

Teaching the three to five year olds.

Some children will start walking at nine months, some will be as late as 15 months. Some children can be good swimmers at two and a half years and some will be only good swimmers at four years. Those parents who have swimming pools or go boating or water skiing should have their children taught as soon as possible. If there is a swimming school nearby, make enquiries first. Make sure that the person who is going to teach your child knows his business. He or she must also have that ability to get on with children.

Young children should not only be taught swimming, they should also be 'drown-proofed'. The teacher may have to employ all sorts of tricks to achieve this but the end result is more than satisfying. Once the parents make up their minds that the child is going to learn to swim, they should persevere, regardless of how long it takes. Progress can't be speeded up. Every child will react differently to instruction.

Children are more receptive after they have had one or two terms at school. By that time they are really eager to learn and what's most important, they have learned how to concentrate and to imitate a teacher.

Theoretically, children are taught to swim by the Education Department, but unfortunately it's not compulsory and I know for a fact that many children miss out. Also, the Department doesn't teach children under six years of age. There should be a drive to get all families, especially migrants, interested in the Education Department's swimming schools.

In the three-to-five age group it is much better to have a stranger to do the teaching. It could be a neighbour, a friend of the family, or best of all, it could be a qualified swimming instructor.

TEACHING THEM YOURSELF
If you yourself want to take up teaching, start off with a small number of pupils. Bad tempered teachers can do more harm

than good. When teaching, don't strive for absolute perfection. The most important thing is the children's happiness and willingness to learn. We can and should all become teachers of something if we are to consider ourselves responsible adults. Swimming and matters of life-saving are very basic to existence in Australia and should involve us all in some way, if we have anything much to do with children. (Remember, I'm not advocating that you should teach in a professional capacity.)

How many children should be in the class?

If you are not experienced or if you are not very sure of yourself, start off with two. I think for an experienced teacher the ideal number is four children in the class.

When dealing with pre-school children, it is much better for them to have company while they are learning something. If you have just one child he or she will tire very quickly and the concentration span will be very short indeed. The ideal situation would be to have a half-hour lesson, after which, a half hour of play.

It all depends on the size of the pool whether you can afford to let them have a romp around. When there are, say, four children in the class, they all have to take their turn. While one gets personal instruction from you, the other three are either resting or playing or practising. This way, of the given half hour, each child gets about seven minutes' individual tuition. That doesn't sound very much, but the trouble is that even if you kept them in the water for, say, two hours they would still only be receptive for about seven to ten minutes.

If the pool is outdoors, you will soon find that the children will start shivering and turn blue, after 20 minutes in the water. It's a funny thing about children that while they are having a lesson they tend to get very cold and miserable very quickly, but the moment you utter the magic words, 'It's playtime', the face which was blue a minute before turns to a rosy red. The same child can stay in the water for practically an unlimited time, just playing.

When you ask them half way through the lesson:

'Are you cold?'

there is a teeth-chattering answer,

Reviewing the children from the outside.

'Yeeeees!'

But if you ask the same question after two hours' play—despite the goose pimples, blue lips, 'crinkly' hands—the answer is,

'No, can we please stay just a little bit longer?'

While children are in class they don't move around very much and in the early stages of their learning they are scared, which is the reason for their shivering. The same child who was getting so cold when you first started to teach him will stop this after a few lessons when he has gained some confidence.

If it is a slightly windy day, keep their shoulders under the water right through the lesson. If they stand or run too much the winds blow through them.

Make it a rule that they never get wet before lesson time. Don't let children in the water before the start of the lesson, even if it's a 98° hot sunny day, because if they have their play first, they are completely useless and worn out for their lesson.

Before entering the water make sure that all children have gone to the toilet and have blown their noses. Be very strict about not letting them have anything in their mouths—lollies and especially chewing gum. If a kid looks suspect ask him to open his mouth so you can examine it. If there is anything in the mouth, it not only distracts their attention, but they can easily bite their tongue.

If you teach very young children you must be prepared to go into the water with them. Even if the teaching takes place in the very shallow end of the pool, you must be right there. If the weather is not to your own liking and you don't feel like going in, rather cancel the lesson than stay outside to give instruction.

Teaching the easy way

There are a few books and pamphlets written on the topic of swimming instruction. Most deal with the subject by giving lesson-by-lesson instructions. The unsuspecting reader gets the impression that it's so easy, just take ten lessons and you are ready for the Olympics! They say, 'First lesson you learn how

'What's your name?'
——silence——
'Would you like to come in the water with me?'
'No.'

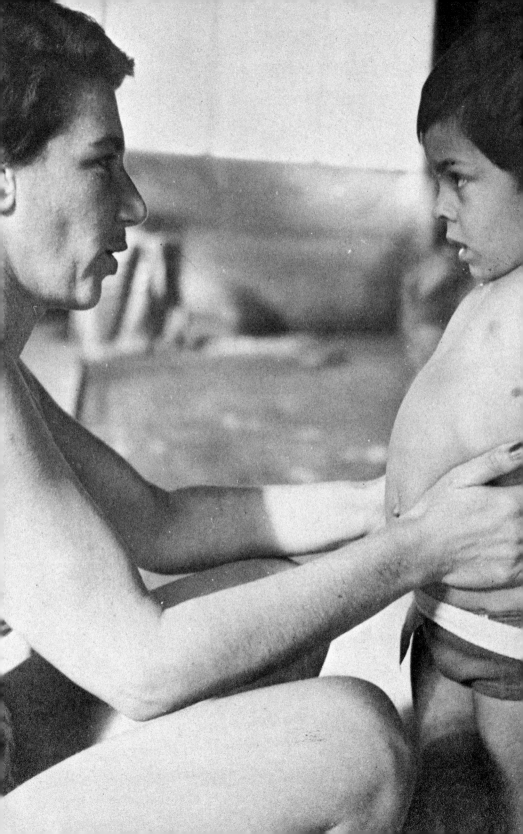

to float; second lesson, you learn how to kick (the generous ones maybe throw in arm movements as well); on the third you learn how to breathe, etc., etc.' It takes at least ten lessons to teach a three-year-old to just float face down! This is why I shall not deal with lesson progress, but explain how I can get a child swimming step-by-step rather than lesson-by-lesson.

Don't ever *demonstrate* swimming to the children. I know this will shock many people; the most accepted method in Australia is to demonstrate. I'm sure we all have watched on television people like Lew Hoad and Ken Rosewall playing tennis, but even if you watch them carefully that's no assurance that you will turn into a Lew Hoad if you have never held a tennis racket before. You must start with the basics.

My teaching method consists of dividing swimming into phases or very simple movements and then, after mastering them one at a time, putting these phases or stages into one. It's no use talking about first lesson, second lesson, etc., because the rate of learning differs from person to person. You might have to spend ages trying to teach a very simple thing to one child whilst another will pick it up immediately. Be patient! And kind!

Big words

When teaching don't use big words. Always remember that your pupils are pre-school age. I remember years ago, I was teaching a four-year-old girl, Julie, to float on her back. She was stiff as an ironing board and I kept on whispering into her ear, 'Relax, Julie, relax'. She looked back at me with a blank, uncomprehending look, and it dawned on me that she didn't know what I was talking about. After the lesson I went over to her father and asked him would he, when they got home, try to explain to her what the word relax means.

Next morning Julie turned up with a big grin on her face and when I asked her, 'Do you know what "relax" means?', she threw herself with a big dramatic movement on the floor, holding her arms and legs indeed in a very relaxed way, eyes closed. I congratulated her on her performance and turned to her father asking, 'How did you do it?'

He said, 'We were watching TV last night and every time

45

Having the egg on tends to make the children kick in an odd way.
Looks like riding a bicycle.

an Indian was shot down, I said to Julie, "See, this is how you relax".'

From that day on I have never used the word 'relax', instead, I say, 'Let yourself go, softly, loose, be a rag-doll, be a jelly.' It works.

Four-year-olds don't understand words like 'submerge', 'surface', 'exhale', 'inhale'; use phrases like go under, come up, blow out, take a big breath. Don't forget, don't lose patience if you have to repeat the same thing a hundred times. When giving an instruction, always use the same expression, the same words; even the facial expressions should be the same. If you say, 'Take a big breath', always take a big breath yourself, over-emphasizing the opening of the mouth.

Perhaps the children in the class are complete strangers to you. They have never seen you, so don't expect that they will put their little arms around your neck, give you a big kiss, and say, 'Please, would you teach me to swim?'

The first and most important thing you have to do is to gain these little strangers' confidence. After all, they are going to place their lives in your hands, and you being a grown up should know that it is not an easy thing to do. If you are running regular classes, it's not a bad idea to ask the parents to bring their children to watch you taking another class, once or twice, before the new children are due to have their first lesson. The children then have an opportunity to size you up, get used to your voice, and see how a swimming lesson is run.

The first time a child comes down, tell him your name and ask him what his name is (even if you know that his name is Mark, John, Tom, etc.). If the child readily answers back and has a conversation with you, you shouldn't expect too much trouble from him. If he doesn't say a word but is quite willing to walk with you to the edge of the pool, he will be a slow starter but later will 'blossom out' into a willing pupil. Yet another one will be crying softly, not making too much of a fuss but letting the world know that she is not terribly happy. And then, of course, there will be the screamer, the yeller, the grabber. Let's call the first one Mark, the second Sandra, the third Tracy and the screamer John.

46

Take Mark and Sandra's hands and start walking in the shallow part of the pool. Keep talking all the time. Keep asking Sandra her name, whether she has any brothers or sisters, if she has a pet in the house, if she goes to kindergarten, what her teacher's name is, and so on. Sooner or later you will find a subject which is very close to her heart and the minute she starts talking back to you, you are friends.

While you are trying to make friends with Mark and Sandra, sit Tracy on the edge of the pool, keep an eye on her but look as if you are ignoring her completely, that you don't even know that she is sitting there. Pick up John, drag him away from mother, and make him sit next to Tracy. By this time Tracy has stopped whimpering and the appearance of John and his screaming makes her start all over again. If John has a bad case of hysterics he might even run back to mother again, so the performance has to be repeated again.

With Mark and Sandra now your friends, sit on the edge of the pool, with John and Tracy on each side of you, holding John's hand firmly—not necessarily for support but rather to hold him back from running to mother again. Start kicking your legs gently in the water. Ask the group if any one can kick their legs similarly. At the first attempt, guess who is going to imitate you?...Mark. At this stage, stand in front of the children and say, 'When I say go, start kicking again.' Even if the splashing is very little, in mock horror say 'Children, please don't splash me!', after which they all start splashing madly. For the first time you can see a devilish smile on Tracy's face and even John is splashing away furiously, so that he can get back at you.

The four magic eggs and four kicking-boards are already on the side of the pool, so 'egg up' Mark and Sandra, give an egg to Tracy to play with, and this time, just look through John as if he is not there. All this should take place on the shallow side of the pool where children can comfortably stand, or even sit.

Take Mark by the hand walking in front of him and gently pull him along to the 3' 6" depth. Here the water comes to your waist but is above the children's heads. Ask Mark to show

49

you if he can kick his legs, which of course he can. Tell him that he is going to learn to swim like a doggie, which will appeal to him very much. If he has a dog at home, ask what the dog's name is and for the rest of the lesson don't call him Mark, but say, 'Come Rover, let's go for a swim'.

Do the same with Sandra and when it's Tracy's turn, don't put the egg on her yet, but hold her, not by the hand, but under the shoulder. Do two or three rounds with the children before you turn to John who, in the meantime, has quietened down, wondering what's going to happen to him, and watching the other children having their turns. Without warning, pick John up under the shoulders and take him along. He will start crying again but the minute you put him down back in the shallow part he will be quiet.

Gradually start moving the children's hands under the water in a circular movement. Half way through the lesson put the egg on Tracy, who by that time is quite willing to do anything, especially after seeing that the other children have come to no harm. With John, just play it by ear. If he calms down enough to have the egg on, put it on by all means, but if he is still playing tiger with you, don't force the issue. John might be carrying on for another two or three lessons, but once he settles down or becomes what I call 'broken in', you will find that he is going to be the quickest to learn of the four.

The reason for all the tantrums is not that he doesn't like the water (mother tells me that in the bathroom he can hold his head under for a long time), but he is strongly objecting to a stranger ordering him about. Very likely, he has not started kindergarten yet and this first swimming lesson is his first encounter with the big, cruel world which exists outside his home.

Having the egg on tends to make the children kick in an odd way. Instead of making a splash on the top of the water they will bend their knees in under their tummies like riding a bicycle or running. There is a reason for this. Not being able to relax they curl up. You know yourself that if you have a cramp or a stomach ache, the most comfortable position is to draw the knees up to the stomach. These children have a new experience in a strange element—water—so naturally, at first, they are frightened and fight their natural buoyancy. If they relaxed their feet would float up.

Having the egg on doesn't help much because the egg is a big bulky lump on their backs. Those children who have spent considerable time in the water and, more important, are willing to put their faces in the water, will be the ones whose legs will float naturally. After taking a few turns across the pool and back, kicking their legs and moving their arms under the water, with your help, of course, it's time to put them on a kicking-board.

Kicking-board

Place their hands on each side of the board with their thumbs on the upper side. Make sure that their arms are always stretched out, the chin is down in the water. On the first round, put your hands over the child's hands. This gives support and helps to pull the child along. If he tends to pull the board in towards his tummy, let the board go with one hand and keep pressing his chest back with the other, so that eventually he will hold his arms straight again.

As you are walking backwards, keep talking to him to take his mind off what he is doing, and slowly work your hands back until you are just holding the end of the board that is nearest to you. Slowly let the board go altogether and say, 'Isn't that lovely? The water holds you up and I'm not even helping.' There is either an angelic smile or a desperate, 'Please hold on to me!', depending on the child. Let him have his way. In the first two or three lessons, it is better to follow the child's instincts as this is the time when he has to learn to trust you. I always make a point of telling the child beforehand, 'I'm going to let you go now'.

There will be children who will just float aimlessly around—usually the younger ones do that. It takes a while for them to realise that, if they want to move from point A to B, they have to kick their legs to get there. By the end of the first lesson, the children should be kicking around with their kicking-boards. From the above mentioned little company, probably it's John who hasn't achieved this, not because he is

51

52, 53 'Don't hold the board that way. Stretch your arms out.'

54, 55 Slowly work the hands back until you are just holding the end of the board.

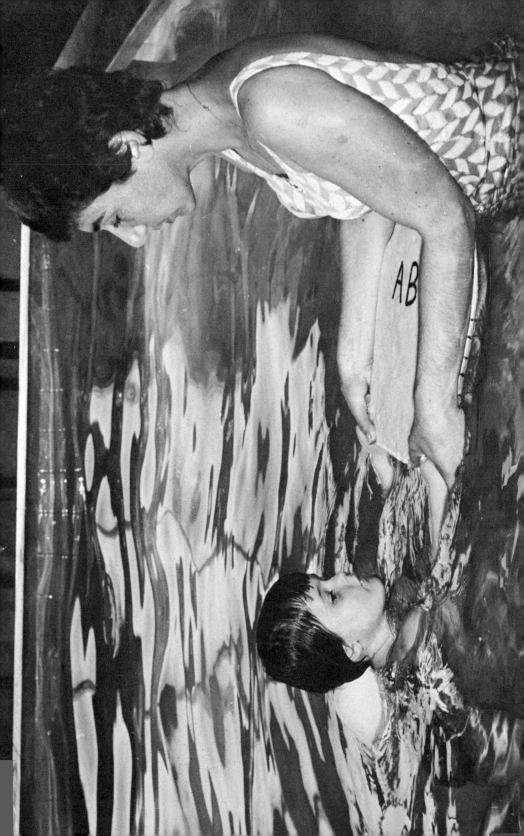

not capable of doing so, but simply because he refused to co-operate.

As you are introducing new things like dog-paddling, kicking, blowing bubbles, holding air, floating, floating on the back, tell the children each time what they are doing. This way they learn the name of each exercise and after a while, if you say 'Let's do some floating on the back', they turn around all by themselves and lean back into your waiting hands. You can save a lot of time by doing this and instead of repeating something a hundred times, at the end, fifty times will be enough.

Dog-paddling

After they have learnt how to kick on the kicking-board, the teacher should go back to the dog-paddling. Holding firmly one of the child's hands say, 'Let this hand go so you try to move this hand all by yourself'. He's going to move it as you showed before in a circular movement. Put your free hand out, hold the other one, and this time shake the other hand free. After a few rounds he will change hands quite freely and willingly. If you feel that he is kicking his legs very steadily while this is going on, without warning shake both of his hands free of yours and let him go on his own.

He will either start swimming, holding his head clear above the water, kicking his legs in the bicycle fashion, moving his hands under the water; or he will start yelling at the top of his voice, 'Don't let me go!' or he will keep kicking but lose his balance by putting his face in the water, in which case you pick him up straight away; or he will just freeze on the spot, forgetting to kick his legs. If he does this he is not ready for free swimming, so back to the kicking-board and the one-arm swimming.

This kind of free paddling can be very deceiving for some parents. They say, 'Good-O, my child can swim'. Unfortunately, this is far from the truth. If you took the egg off, these children, at this stage, would sink like a rock. Children are free and safe swimmers only if they can swim in a horizontal position, head under the water and coming up for air.

56

'This is how a doggie swims. It's called dog-paddling.'

58 *'Let one hand go, and try to move this hand all by yourself.'*

59 *He will soon be keeping himself afloat.*

Why use the egg?

You may ask why bother teaching them with an egg? To start a two-year-old swimming, it would take ages to get him to swim on his own if you didn't have the egg—it just makes things much easier. Normally, a child would first have to learn to float but this can be by-passed by attaching an egg in the first place. In this way you have a child swimming on his own in four or five lessons. For a child who hasn't yet learnt how to put his face into the water, swimming around, even though supported by an egg, gives him a great freedom, and very early in his learning he can feel he has achieved something. For those people who have a swimming pool at home, this can be a great help. A child who can only swim when he has an egg on realises this and wouldn't dream of going into the water without it.

At the end of each lesson make sure that the egg is taken off for a short while and make the child do something without it. Find out what he likes to do best, e.g., kicking on the board, floating on the back, etc., and do that particular exercise with him, *without the egg.* It's a good idea to take the eggs off for playtime (unless the swimming pool hasn't a shallow end).

Teachers should try putting an egg on to test the buoyancy. If you are a strong swimmer, you will find that you can hardly feel the egg on your back. The reason for this is that you are floating so high on the surface of the water that it is impossible to feel the lift. When somebody is tense in the water or lets his feet drop, then the full holding-up power can be felt.

Blowing bubbles

To get a child used to being completely under the water, it takes a long, tedious, nerve-racking, time-consuming period. First, you ask them to show you if they can blow a bubble. Nine out of ten can do it once they know what is required. For the one child who doesn't know how to do it, the best thing is to take their hand and blow hard on the wet surface. From that they feel the air on their hand and they get an idea what 'blow' means. Another way is to ask, 'How do you blow out your birthday candles?'

So they can feel the impact of the air coming through the

Take a bi-i-i-g breath and bubble.

water, put your hands cupped underneath their mouths so that when they blow they can see it, hear it and feel it.

There are two things that children have to learn to do in the water. One is to blow and breathe regularly, commonly known as 'blowing bubbles'. The other is not to let the air out, but hold it for a given time.

When you want them to put their faces in and hold their breath, you say *every time,* 'Take a big breath, close your mouth and I'm going to count five, seven (whatever the case may be)'. Not only do you have to repeat the instruction *every* single time but when saying, 'Take a big breath', you yourself should take an enormous breath, too. Or, if you say, 'Open your mouth', you open your mouth so much that the children can see your tonsils.

Don't ask the impossible. If you are just starting off with three seconds under the water and you know the child can hardly do it, don't say, 'Now that you have held it for three, let's try and make it ten'. By the way, when somebody's head is under the water they can still hear sounds from 'outside'.

When holding the breath insist on the eyes and ears being under the water. It is too early at this stage to ask them to open their eyes under the water. This will come later. If you are having difficulty in getting the head under the water during the lesson, this is where helpful and intelligent parents come in.

For instance, there are a few methods which could be practised with parent supervision at home:
1. Face in the water (bathtub) holding their breath up to the count of five or more.
2. Blowing bubbles at regular intervals.
3. Opening eyes under the water. (Show coloured objects under the water, dive for cent pieces.)
4. Alternate between having a shower and a bath. The shower shouldn't be full on, but insist on the child being right underneath. Give plastic bottles to fill, wash dolly's hair under the shower, etc.

Once a child can hold his breath without trouble, without effort, he is ready to learn to float. The expression 'deadman's float' I never use, as it has a very sinister sound to it. Can you

63

'Look Mummy, I can blow bubbles.'

imagine a bright kid asking 'What's a deadman's float?' Then you will have to say, 'That's how you float when you drown and you are dead'.

Learning to float

If the water is shallow, a good method is to have the children kneel down, arms outstretched, take a deep breath and gently fall forward. Or, if the water is above their heads, hold their arms, making sure that their legs are outstretched and that they are lying flat on top of the water. The first time you do that, tell the child, 'I want you to take a deep breath, put your face in the water. I'm going to count to five and will let you go while you are under the water, and when you run out of breath I'm going to fish you out'.

By this time the relationship between the teacher and pupil should be so good that the child will know that he can trust the teacher and that if she says 'I will fish you out', she really means it. The best way to do this is to have the child touch your shoulders while your free hands are supporting his hips. At the word 'Go' he goes under, lets your shoulders go a couple of inches, and for a few short seconds he feels the sensation of floating for the first time in his life.

If it went off without a hitch, praise him like mad. Repeat this a few times then let him stand in the shallow part of the pool and you should stand back in the deeper part, at first just a few feet away. Hold your arms out, ready to catch him, and say, 'You try to float here to me'. As time goes on you can increase the distance.

The next step is to get them paddling with their faces in the water. The big drawback will be that they are used to having the egg on their backs, so they will still tend to kick their legs downwards.

Tell them to take a deep breath, face in the water, move their arms in a circular movement and kick their legs. You walk backwards away from them and, as you do, you create a vacuum in front of you. The quicker you walk the bigger the vacuum will be. The children are sucked into it and it gives them a much greater speed than if they swam entirely on their own.

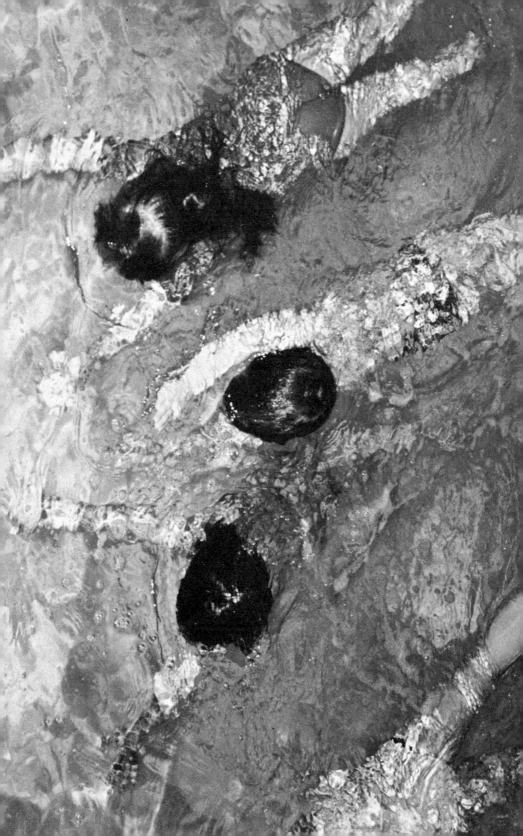

When you feel they need to come up for air, lift the head above the water by putting a hand under the chin. After taking a breath they should go down again and keep repeating this until they get used to the idea. With this age group, I still don't insist on blowing bubbles out or holding their breath. Some will blow out, some will hold onto it, so that when they come up to the surface they will let the air out before inhaling again. This is the time when a teacher needs to have ten arms instead of two. There are so many faults to correct, which should be rather done by touch than by verbal instruction.

If the legs are trailing too low, lift them up a bit by pushing their hips up. If they tend to splash out with their arms, push the arms down. If they forget to come up for air, give a little tap on the top of the head or lift the chin up, and so on, and so on.

This should be done without their eggs on. Some children get a little too game at this stage so, as you are taking one child at a time, keep looking back continually at the other three. If one child keeps on jumping into the deep end and has difficulty in getting back to the shallow part, put an egg on as a safety measure and then take the egg off when he is getting personal instruction from you.

Please don't discourage the children from having little tryouts on their own. Don't ridicule them if they can't get back on their own to the edge of the pool. Just walk over nonchalantly and lift them up without saying a word.

Opening eyes under water

At this stage they are ready to learn how to open their eyes under the water. While floating you can say, 'Try to open your eyes under the water and see if you can see my swimming costume'. They come up very excitedly, and say, 'I saw your costume, it's black and white'. After this you can have a little game with all the four children sitting on the side. Say, 'I'm going to show you my fingers under the water and you tell me how many fingers you see'. Get the brightest child to have a go first and when he puts his face in (holding his breath), put your outstretched fingers right under his face. Depending on the children's age, show one or two fingers for the young

67

The arms resting on my shoulders.

ones and three to five for the older ones.

If you have very young children who can't recognise numbers or even colours, get two different coloured plastic discs, or, for that matter, any similar object, in your hands and say, 'I'm going to show you this (red) or that (blue)'. The little ones go under the water, have a look and they will point and will say, 'I saw that (blue)'.

Another good way of opening their eyes is for both the teacher and pupil to go under the water together and look into each other's eyes. After a while you can make funny faces at each other, which is tremendous fun.

After learning to float, the teacher should pick one child at a time and, holding them under the shoulders, push them down under the water. You have to know how long each individual child in your class can stay under the water. Once the child is deep down, gently let the grip go and let him come up on his own. This is the way to learn how to swim in deep water.

Don't forget that a depth of 3' 6", where an adult can comfortably stand, is as deep to a three-year-old child as 6' 6" is to an adult. By the same token, if a three-year-old has learnt and can swim in a 3' 6" pool, you can easily let him swim in a 6' 6" depth or in a bottomless lake. Deep water is deep water and once you have learnt to swim in it, it doesn't matter where you do it.

Once they can sit on the bottom of the pool, holding their breath, then they can learn to let the air out, to blow a bubble. Hold them by the shoulders, push them under the water, let them blow *all* the air out, then lift their heads out, let them take a *big* breath and push them under the water again. If they tend to touch their eyes with their hands or shake their heads, hold their hands firmly so they can't. Push them up and down in a regular rhythmic movement. They must learn to open their eyes as soon as their faces come out of the water. Nobody should be allowed to swim with their eyes shut. One loses one's balance and sense of direction and, when you swim, you can't afford that. Imagine crossing a busy street with your eyes shut!

The child is pulled by the vacuum.

Going stale

How quickly a child is progressing at this stage depends not on how many lessons he has had but on how much supervised playtime he gets. I know from personal experience that children can stagnate at this stage (they can swim with the teacher's aid but not by themselves), but, if the family happens to go away for a two-week holiday where the children spend a considerable time in the water, they come back strong and independent swimmers.

In the three-to-five-year age group it can also happen that children are simply not progressing at all. In these cases it doesn't do any harm for them to stop having lessons for a while. Take a six-month rest. When these children come back again, they are six months older, they have grown, got stronger and their ability to learn has improved. Thank goodness that once you have learnt something in the water you will never forget it, so they can take six months off and pick up where they left off.

When children can swim about six to ten yards on their own, you should stay out of the water for one lesson, pretending that you have a sore tummy or a cold. You should still be in a swimming costume and sit on the edge of the pool, then ask the children to go through their paces—blowing bubbles on the side, holding their breath on the side, kicking on the board and then dog-paddling a given distance.

Some children will refuse to swim without the teacher being right there in the water with them. This is very disappointing for the teacher and the parents, but the teacher should be very firm and make the child swim on his own for a little distance, even if it means that he has to be gently shoved into the water. The child has to learn to be independent. He might cry, but you must insist. The trouble is that young children get so used to the teacher. They have put so much trust in her that they simply cannot imagine doing things without her being right there within 'grabbing' distance.

Children tend to feel more secure in the particular swimming pool where they first learnt to swim. This can be a problem. I have known children to drag their parents as much as ten

This little boy didn't blow his bubbles out under the water.

They must learn to breathe out under water.

Pushing the child under the water.

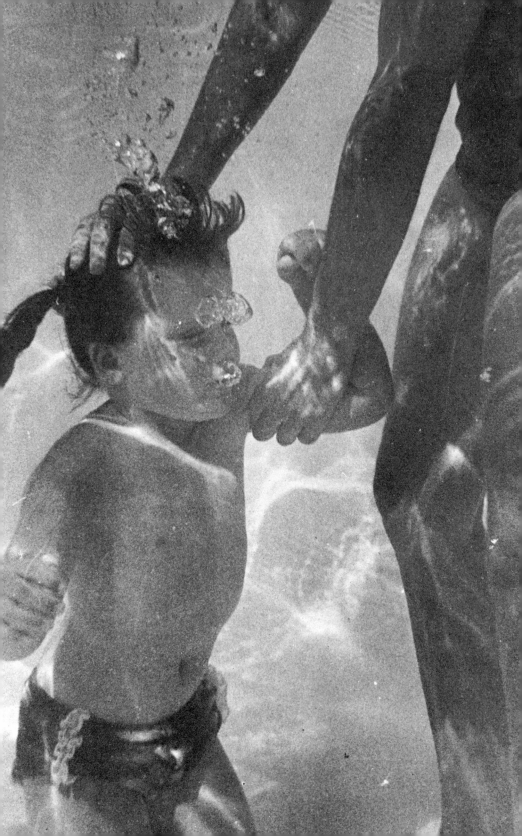

miles to the particular swimming pool where they first learnt to swim, rather than going nearby to a similar size pool and surroundings. If a child is too attached to the teacher and swimming pool, the parents should make a trip to another swimming pool and prove that the child can swim *anywhere*.

How often I have heard from desperate parents after a weekend's outing, 'He wouldn't do a thing for us'. This, of course, happens quite often, but parents have to persevere and make their children do what they know they are capable of doing. Of course I am not advocating that children be thrown into the pool. To throw a non-swimmer into the water, in my mind, is terrible. One child out of ten will probably swim out quite unharmed, but the other nine will have such a fright that they may never get rid of their fear. However, I do insist on making children do what they have been taught, no more, and no less. If one child had 20 lessons and can swim and jump in my pool, I would certainly expect him to show mummy and daddy how he can float.

Kicking on the back
To teach the three-to-five-year age group floating and kicking on their backs, the same method should be employed as teaching the babies. Teach them to float first, standing always behind them, supporting their heads in one hand, correcting the body position by touch until they float, completely horizontal and relaxed. The teacher should walk backwards and pull the child along in the vacuum which she has created. The kicking shouldn't be too powerful, rather get the balance and movement by moving the arms under the water. Once this is learnt, the teacher can show the class how to turn from kicking on the back to dog-paddling and from dog-paddling to kicking on the back.

Jumping and diving
The children should be introduced to jumping into the water almost as soon as they start to learn to swim. For those children who are absolutely petrified of putting their faces in the water, jumping in should be delayed. However, any child who can blow bubbles and can hold his face in the water, even if it is

Floating on the back. Notice the girl in the middle—how relaxed her hands are.

76, 77 Pulled by the vacuum.

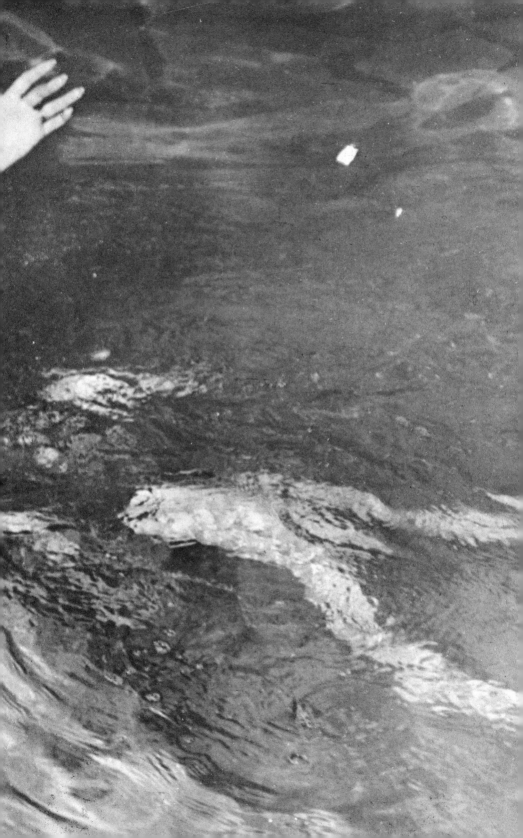

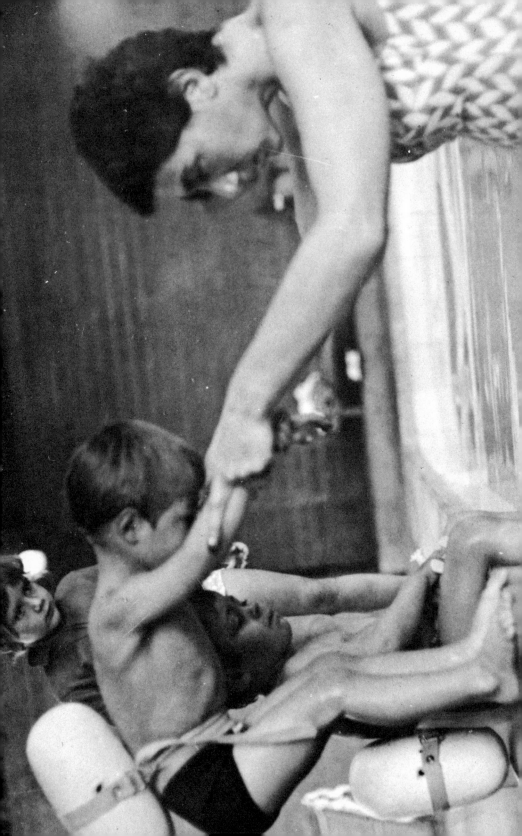

only for a short time, should be made to jump.

Sit the children on the edge of the pool, tell them to stretch their arms out and at the word 'go' gently pull them into the water. On the very first attempt the teacher shouldn't let their hands go because she will have to help them find their balance, as they come up to the surface.

Now, make them stand on the edge of the pool and repeat the same procedure by pulling them in by the hand. After a couple of goes, stand back two steps and try to make them do it on their own. The brave ones will jump as if they had been doing it all their lives. But the not-so-brave will look at you with pleading eyes which seem to say 'What are you trying to do to me? Teacher, come a bit closer'.

'No, you try to do it alone. When you get into the water I will fish you out.'

'But I can't do it. I'm scared!'

'When I say "Ready . . . go", you jump.'

'I caaaan't!'

This can go on for five minutes, with the poor child deciding he will do it, then at the last moment, changing his mind. It's worth waiting for the Big Moment. The decision has to come from the child, so it is not much good giving him a shove. Needless to say, after that first jump he will turn around and do it again, and again, and again. If the child is not advanced enough, all the jumping, and later on diving, could be done with the egg on.

To teach the children to dive, line them up at the edge of the pool. Making sure that their feet are slightly apart, the toes curling onto the very edge of the pool, knees bent. Arms should be stretched up above their heads, which are tucked down.

For the first dive, the teacher should stand beside the child and place one hand on his head (holding it down) and his other hand on the bottom. With a powerful movement, 'whack' them into the water. For the second attempt, the teacher should ask the children if they want some 'help' or if they want to do it on their own. Some will say 'I can do it' and some will sheepishly look at you and say 'Yes, please, help me'.

79

The First Jump—with an anxious onlooker.

80, 81   Ready . . .

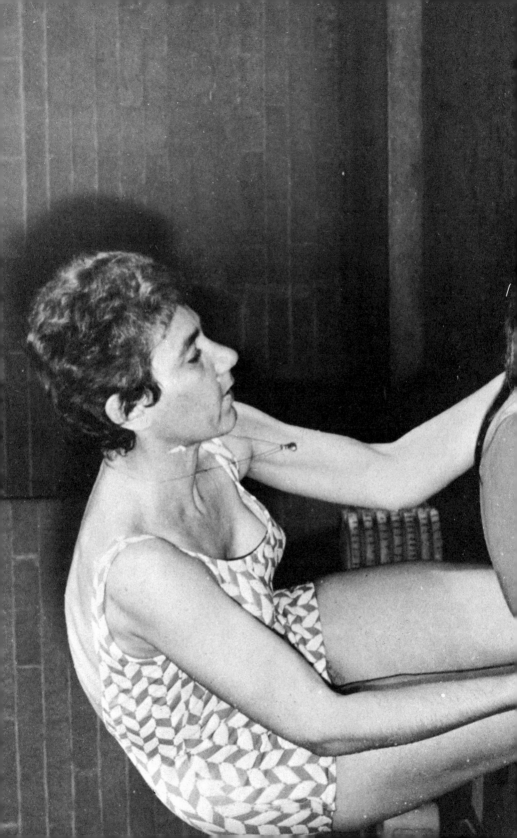

The individual style is quite amazing. Some will do a belly-flopper, some will start off as if they are going to dive but half way through the air change to a jump. And then, occasionally, some will perform a perfect swallow dive. At this age the teacher shouldn't correct the clumsy divers. Let them do what they feel like doing. There is plenty of time for improving technique later on.

Jumping and diving without an egg on is only advisable when children can swim at least five or six yards. Once children have started diving, they will want to do it forever and they will do it when you are not watching, so it is better to make sure that they can swim on their own to the edge of the pool.

Go!
84, 85 This perfect dive is done by a four-year-old!

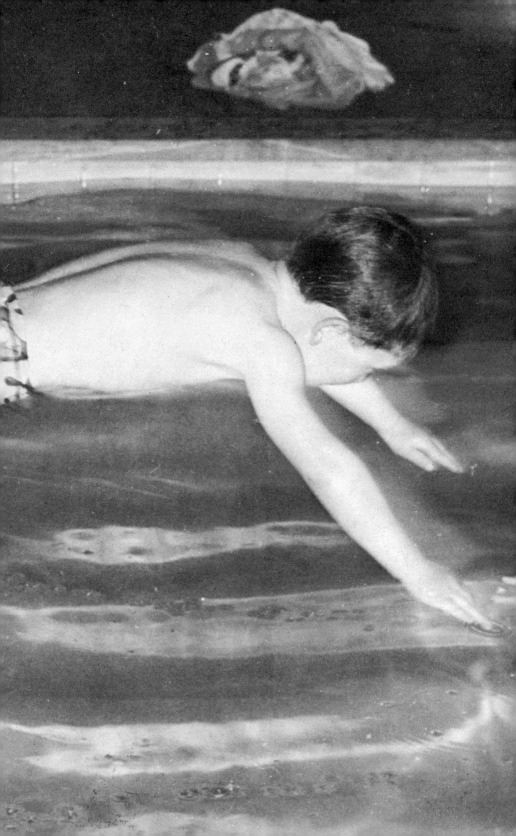

Five to ten year olds-advanced swimming.

In this chapter I am going to deal with teaching a child or adult an efficient freestyle. The following teaching method could be used with a three-or-four-year-old, provided that he is already very familiar with the water. One cannot by-pass stages so, when one has learnt to float and dog-paddle, it is time to learn freestyle.

For this chapter I am assuming that when the children come for tuition, they can already float and thrash along in some fashion. The chapter heading may be misleading. It does not in any way mean that if a child has turned five he should immediately be taught freestyle.

To start off, children have to learn how to push and glide. The teacher should stand back from the children a couple of yards and say, 'Arms up, take a deep breath and glide over to me'. After that, they can do push-and-glide with kicking. When they are not facing the teacher, they should be instructed to stand back from the wall and practise going towards it. When the teacher wants to increase the distance, she should step back one step at a time, or tell the children to stand further away from the wall. It is not a good idea to stand them against the wall and say 'Kick as far as you can go', because when children know exactly how far they are expected to go, they make a great effort to get there. If they are allowed to stop anywhere they will give up more easily.

Before commencing the arm movements, the teacher should demonstrate how to move one arm in a circle. When demonstrating, hold the arm stiffly straight, horizontally and in front, fingers pointed, palms down. Swing the arm down to the leg then sweep it back behind as far as it will go, then bring the arm up and over slowly without bending the elbow. Children should do this standing out of the water, moving one arm first, then the other. When they are moving their arms correctly, holding them straight, they can practise moving them continuously.

86

87, 88, 89, 91   Look back on your breathing arm.

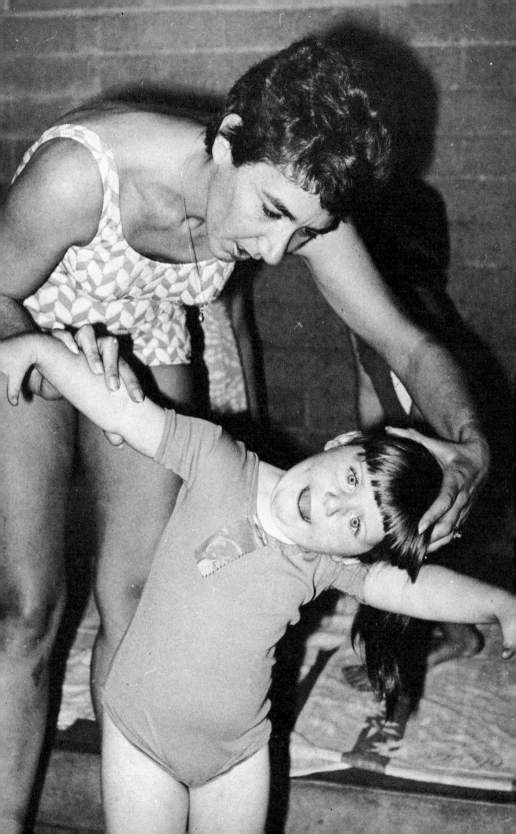

Why should the arms be straight?

The correct crawl stroke is, of course, done by bending the elbows slightly over the water with the tips of the fingers touching the water first, followed by a firm but bent wrist. My many years of teaching experience has taught me that if one shows a child a slightly bent elbow they over-emphasize the movement. Their arms enter the water at too sharp an angle, 45°, which, of course, cuts the freestyle stroke in half. By showing a straight-arm entry, they get the feeling of stretching out in front, reaching down into the water and thus achieving an economical stroke technique. As they are progressing they loosen up and, without anybody telling them, they begin to bend their arms naturally, so that they finish up swimming a relaxed and correct freestyle stroke. If a child, by some miracle, looks as if he is going to do this, for goodness sake don't tell him to keep his arms straight, but, believe me, this doesn't happen often.

After showing them how to move their arms, tell them to 'Take a deep breath, put your face in the water and swim *slowly* to me, moving your arms.' Have them do this a few times before you start correcting them. Look under the water and watch their arms and how they pull.

If the child doesn't pull down on the centre line of his body, correct this by showing him the angle he is doing it, then show him the correct angle. Tell him to open his eyes under the water and watch his hands going down. He can see for himself what you are talking about: whether his arms go down straight or slip out to the side. The teacher can say, 'If you pull out to the side, you are pushing the water away from you, but if you are pulling your arms straight down you are pushing the water underneath you'. (By the way, it's an old wives' tale that the fingers should be pressed hard against each other and that it is a capital sin to have the fingers open.) Then watch carefully that nobody swims with a bent and collapsed elbow.

Breathing

When doing freestyle one turns the head to breathe. The side you breathe on is determined by whether one is right-handed

or left-handed. Right-handed people find it easier to turn their heads to the right side, left-handed people find it easier to turn them to the left side.

Get a texta colour and paint a dot on the child's hand. When doing this ask which hand he holds his pencil in at school. As you put the dot on declare that this, from now on, is going to be his *Breathing Arm.* If a child is too small to know which hand he holds his pencil in, the safest way to find out whether right- or left-handed is to ask mother.

Never talk about right or left, just call the spotted hand, 'breathing arm' and the plain one, 'the other arm'. Keep putting the spot on until such time that when you ask the child, 'Which is your breathing arm?' they automatically lift that up. It is rather funny to see a child looking at his clean hand, lifting one at a time to his eyes, trying to remember which one had the dot on. Using the texta colour, which doesn't wash off easily, helps greatly because after they go home from their swimming lesson they carry the dot on their hands for hours, reminding them all the time 'This is my breathing arm'. You will find that the younger they are, the more proudly they wear this mark.

When explaining, for the first time, let the children come out of the water and show them individually what you want them to do. 'When your breathing arm comes out of the water, you turn your head back, look back on it and take a b-i-i-i-g breath. When your breathing arm goes into the water, you put your head in and blow b-i-i-i-g bubbles.' As you explain this, stand behind each child, hold the breathing arm in your right hand while the left hand is on the top of the child's head. This way you can synchronize the head movements with the arms. Keep telling them to look back at their breathing arm, putting their chin on their shoulder as they breathe in, then instead of letting the head come up, roll the chin down to the chest as they blow out.

When teaching outdoors, it would be a good idea to let the children do the land drill before they enter the water, otherwise you might have four shivering children, unable to attend to you because they are cold.

If the children are tall enough to stand up comfortably in the 3′ 6″ end of the pool, make them walk a certain distance, practising the above mentioned drill, but this time make them put their faces into the water to blow the bubbles. This walking is a very good way of getting them to co-ordinate the movements, because if they make a mistake they can hear your instruction to correct it more easily than if they were already swimming. Funnily enough, the mistakes they do walking, e.g., bending arms, not lifting left arm when blowing out, jerking the head up, holding onto their breath, etc., they will do when swimming.

If the pool has a fair amount of shallow space in it, they can do a 'crocodile walk': both hands touching the bottom of the pool, legs stretched out completely, they start walking on their hands. As the breathing arm comes out, they turn their heads back and take a big breath. When the other arm comes out, they blow out a big bubble. If the children are not tall enough to touch bottom, or if there is not a sufficient area of shallow to practise in, the teacher should take one child at a time and do the following.

If, say, the child is right-handed so he is breathing on the right side, the teacher should stand on the child's left. In your right hand hold the child's right elbow (to prevent bending the arm back). In your left hand, hold the child's left elbow. When first starting off you should lift the left knee up, to support the child under his side, and place the head in a flat position. The left ear has to be under the water and the top of the head as well. Holding the breathing arm down, say, 'This is when you have to take a big breath'. Slowly start walking, moving the child's arms so that he has to concentrate only on turning his head and breathing. Reaching the end of the pool, everybody turns around. At this time ask, 'Now, which way will you turn your head?' The child will look at his hands and after great consultation look at his breathing arm and say, 'This way.'

When you think of it, turning the head to one particular side only is a very confusing matter. What you look at changes. When you are swimming down the length of the pool you keep breathing toward the fence. But when you come back you are

not looking at the fence, but at the house. If you have the mark on your hand it makes it easier to tell when you should be looking at the fence and when at the house.

When the children have a fair idea of how and when to turn their heads, and when to breathe in and out, the teacher should stand in front of each child and make him swim after her.

Holding the child's left hand in one hand, let him take a breath, make a full circle with his breathing arm, and then only catch his left in the front for support. This method could be applied if the child is thrashing the water or moves his arms too quickly. It slows him down so that he can breathe in and out, at a much more leisurely pace.

FAULTS TO WATCH FOR

Too much kicking: Some children are very flexible at the ankles and before coming to you for lessons they may have spent a whole summer doing kicking-board work and nothing else. So, when they start learning freestyle, the kicking has been over-practised and they have yet to learn to co-ordinate the arm movements with the leg movements.

The secret of breathing is to do it slowly, allowing enough time for the lungs to expand and contract. Too much kicking will thrust the body forward, not allowing the arms to go around in a slow, relaxed way; the child will consequently tend to move his arms much too fast. Tell the child to see if he can swim *without kicking his legs at all!* If he tries very hard he will be able to do it; the arms will go much slower and he will have sufficient time to breathe in and out.

Actually his feet do not drag behind but kick at a much slower pace. The child honestly believes that he didn't kick at all, so let him believe it and don't say, 'Aha . . . you were still kicking your legs when I asked you not to!' If he is doing what you want, over the next few lessons, just tell him, 'Remember, try not to kick your legs so you can go very slowly.'

Not enough kicking: Some children seem as if they are only dragging their feet and when put on a kicking-board they don't seem to be able to move at all. They are probably kicking

Lift the 'other' arm up.

from the knees, instead of the hips.

Some children have enormous chests and very strong arms. When they swim, they propel themselves through the water using their arms only. Murray Rose, the famous Australian swimmer, had a most irregular style. Instead of using a 'normal' six-beat kick he was using an 'abnormal' combination of a two-beat and a four-beat kick. (A six-beat kick is six kicks to one complete arm circle.) He was very powerfully built and used his legs only as a balance to his powerful arm stroke.

Every action has a reaction. If you pick up a heavy bucket full of water and carry it a certain distance, the other arm will automatically spring up as a balance. In swimming, kicking serves as a balance to breathing. When the swimmer turns even slightly for air, his body loses its balance because of the change of position, so the opposite leg will kick out slightly more.

I remember having a pupil called Mathew who came to my swimming school for style correction. He was swimming a very pretty stroke, having spent the previous four or five years in his own backyard pool. Mathew had taken up swimming as a sport and spent the summer training every day with me at an outdoor, Olympic-size pool. Half way through the season, Mathew's father came to me and, horrified, he showed me how his son's pretty six-beat kick turned into an ugly two-beat kick. I had to explain to him that doing two to three miles in a practice session had built up his upper body. When not flat out he used the two-beat kick, but in sprints his kicking speed increased to six-beats.

When children are not kicking a lot, don't be alarmed. If they are swimming along, moving at a reasonable speed, give them plenty of kicking-board work. From a lot of kicking practice they will eventually get the knack of kicking. Just remember they might become another Murray Rose.

Holding the breath: Until somebody has mastered the breathing technique, it's definitely easier to swim along just holding onto your breath and not letting it out. The trouble is that sooner or later one has to stop.

Some children will look as if they are breathing in and out; they open their mouths wide when turning their heads to the side and at the right time they roll their heads back into the water. Children are very good actors and imitators, but the teacher with a sharp eye will be able to see if the child *really* lets the air out. If the pool where you are teaching is not a long one, say 30 or 40 feet long, a child might even swim from one end to the other and appear to be breathing properly. If he is breathing out properly you will see the bubbles.

To correct this particular breathing fault, the teacher should do an exercise which is called 'One-Arm Breathing'. One arm is placed on the top of a kicking-board leaving the other, the breathing arm, to move alone. Say, 'Turn your head, look back when you're breathing out, take a b-i-i-i-g breath, and as your breathing arm goes into the water, blow a b-i-i-i-g bubble out'. If necessary, have the child do this for a couple of lessons.

Alternatively, the child should do a lot of kicking on the kicking-board, holding onto it with both hands, lifting the head up but not too far out of the water, taking a big breath, then blowing a bubble into the water. When coming up for air, leave the chin on the water and when blowing out make sure that the ears are well and truly under the water. If a child is very young and can't understand what you are saying, place your hand under his mouth as he blows out so he can feel the impact of the air hitting the hand. Praise him when you feel the bubbles.

Stopping after three strokes: Your prize pupil suddenly develops a bad habit of stopping after three strokes. You look at him right and you look at him left. You climb out of the water to see if you can pick a fault from there, you ask him if he feels all right, has he got a tummy-ache, and then in desperation you throw your arms up: 'I can't find any fault in him! Why on earth does he stop after every three strokes?'

There is nothing wrong with him . . . he is lazy! If the teaching takes place in a shallow pool, where he can touch bottom, he will find the easy way out and put his foot down the minute he feels tired. If the swimming pool has a deep water area, transfer him there immediately and continue the lessons there for a while. In the deep water his style will suffer a bit, but at least he will swim from one end of the pool to the other.

If there is no deep water facility, you can put a pair of flippers on him and make him swim with them. The flipper gives him enormous speed which in turn gives him added confidence. When he does the fourth stroke after doing the three-stroke-stop, three-stroke-stop, this is the major breakthrough, and from then on he will go on and on.

Another way of overcoming this laziness is for the teacher to put the egg back on him again, even if he is a healthy ten-year-old. Walking by the side of him, the teacher can then give him a good push along by the egg at the critical moment, when he is just about ready to stop.

Left-arm dragging: So much attention is given to the vital co-ordination of breathing and the breathing arm stroke, that it is no wonder the other arm becomes neglected.

Children who find it hard to master the breathing will probably be rolling too much on their left side and therefore will hardly be using the left arm at all. In bad cases they may even roll onto their backs. There is a tendency in everybody to use one arm and one leg more than the other. If the fault is not too bad, leave it alone for a while, and go back to correcting it once the breathing has been mastered. In the next chapter, I will deal with bi-lateral breathing, which is an absolutely marvellous way to get rid of this lopsidedness.

In the early learning stages there is one good method which can be used to get the left arm moving. Put the breathing arm on top of the kicking-board, and move the left arm around only, but this time the head *does not go into the water.* Make sure that the child lifts his left arm very high out of the water and that, on entry, it goes straight down and does not pull out on the side.

Lifting the head out of the water: This is one fault which everybody has in the early learning stages. The child rolls his head and looks back at his breathing arm but, instead of keeping his chin down to finish blowing out, at the last moment, he jerks his head out in front. This is very bad.

The swimmer should be in a flat position and if the head lifts up out of the water the balance is gone. Like a see-saw,

the minute the head comes up, the feet will have to come down. This lifting of the head out front happens in cases where children don't open their eyes or are asthmatic. When the eyes are closed, it is natural to want to see where one is going, so instead of opening the eyes under the water, or during breathing when the face is out of the water on the side, the swimmer leaves it until the last moment. Asthmatic children hate the feeling of their faces being under the water. They have a claustrophobic feeling and are prone to panic, fearing they won't be able to lift their heads out of the water in time to take another breath.

To correct the lifting of the head out front, the children should do a lot of the crocodile walk, the teacher walking along beside them, guiding the head movement with his hands. Again, one-arm breathing can be practised, making sure that the chin touches the shoulder, then rolls down to the chest and back again.

Can't get rid of the air: I often hear it from my adult pupils, 'When I put my face into the water, I somehow can't get rid of the air'.

It can happen to many people, children too. The time allowed between strokes is just not long enough to get rid of the air. In these cases it's advisable to teach breathing on every four strokes.

For the normal freestyle, one takes a breath every time the breathing arm comes out of the water, and blows out when the other arm goes over. Breathing on every fourth stroke means that one takes a breath when the breathing arm comes out and holds it for the next three strokes. Remember, the counting starts when an arm reaches out in front, so it goes—Take a breath—that's one—face in the water—two, three, four—then take a breath again, face in the water—two, three, four.

There are two ways of getting rid of the air for this four-stroke style:
1. To let the air out slowly, bit by bit, carefully enconomising to make it last through the four strokes.
2. To hold onto it, until the very last stroke, and let it out, with a big blow, and then to take a breath in the normal way.

When first introducing breathing on every fourth stroke, it is advisable to let the pupils walk in shoulder-deep water, practising breathing on every four. This way everybody can experiment on which of the two methods of breathing suits them best.

Doing freestyle with a little bit of dog-paddling: Many children are not strong enough to swim correct freestyle straight away. They will roll their heads to their breathing arms, they will bring their arms straight out of the water, they won't jerk their heads up in front, but, as they are pulling their breathing arms under the water, getting ready to take a breath, they will do two little dog-paddles and then continue to stroke.

As they get stronger they will drop the habit or if it worries the teacher or mother, a child could have an egg on again for a while. With the egg on, they can relax and do not have to struggle to do the correct stroke.

Not strong enough: We have many three-and-four-year-olds in our swimming school doing freestyle. Some of them are capable of doing as much as one quarter of a mile non-stop. The majority of them, though they are capable of doing free-style, are not strong enough to do more than five or six strokes. They tire very easily and consequently their style suffers. To overcome this, I have been putting the magic egg on them. They don't need it in the same way the beginners do, but it gives them a little lift and help; so instead of struggling they are able to relax more and concentrate on swimming 'pretty'. The egg can be used on all the children to master the finer points of freestyle. There is less chance of developing bad habits. When the swimmer is strong enough to take the egg off, do it by all means.

Ugly style: The swimmer's style is not pretty, in fact, the style is ghastly! The child looks as if he has ten arms, twenty legs and at least five heads. He doesn't know what to do, splashes wildly, but somehow he manages to beat all other children in a swimming race.

The teacher should try to analyse if there is anything technically wrong with him, but if the answer is 'no', leave him alone. With more practice, it is likely that he will smooth

102, 103 This is freestyle, believe it or not; she has turned nearly on her back as she takes a breath.

his bad habits out.

On the other hand, he could be an ugly swimmer for the rest of his life. Many of the world's great swimmers have been ugly stylists whilst their performances, of course, were great. So don't let it worry you, provided the technique is all right.

SWIMMING DRILLS
On the kicking-board
Kicking.
Kicking, blowing bubbles, lifting the head vertically.
Kicking, blowing bubbles, turning head to the side.
One-arm breathing.
Putting right hand on the board and moving left arm only.
No kicking-board
Crocodile walk
Walking in shoulder-deep water
Doing breathing and bubbling
Swimming with flippers on
Swimming with egg on

LAND DRILLS
Practising arm movement and co-ordination of arms and breathing.

DEEP WATER TREATMENT
Many children will jump into deep water without bothering much about the consequences. They will either panic or just swim out. The majority of them have to be carefully guided into the art of treading water.

If children are taken for the first time into the deep part of the pool, I proceed as follows. The four children in the class all sit down on the edge of the pool and the teacher eases them, one by one, into the water, each child holding onto the edge of the pool. Once all four are in the water, the teacher gives the command to take a big breath, put their faces in the water and hold the breath for five to ten seconds.

With each child in turn, the teacher kneels on the side of the pool and, holding him firmly by the hand, pushes him vertically down. The teacher should name each child, saying first, 'Come on, John, I'm going to hold onto your hands, I'm not going to let them go and I will push you down. Make sure not to blow any bubbles out and to open your eyes'.

After several 'duckings', the teacher should encourage the child to try to do it on his own. By this time he has felt the force which brings him up to the surface of the water, so there shouldn't be much protesting. Some children will still cling to the edge of the pool while they push themselves under, and some of them will have gained enough confidence to let go of the wall. Repeat this ducking about twenty times, then get the children out of the water and make them sit on the edge.

Taking one at a time, ease them back into the water and ask them to dog-paddle or do freestyle (whichever they can do the best) along the wall for about three or four yards. After completing the distance, praise them and comment on how easy it was and how it feels not a lot different from swimming in the shallow pool. Make the children do this at least ten times before you get into the water.

If the teacher is not a strong swimmer, he should find a spot in the swimming pool where he can still comfortably stand, say, four to five feet in depth; for children that depth is still deep. Stand back three to five yards away from the wall and ask one child at a time to swim out to you and back. As they improve, the teacher can ask them to swim around him and then back.

Next take the group of children over to the deepest part of the swimming pool and stand them in a line. Now they will have to jump in one by one. In Olympic-size pools the deepest part is usually 6' 6" and at the very end of the pool there is usually a ladder. If the deep water treatment is done in an Olympic pool, take the children down there and do the jumping at the deep end corner. If it is in a private swimming pool, try to find a similar spot, so that after jumping and coming up they can reach the ladder immediately.

Before proceeding to the big 'First Jump', warn them that the water is deep and the first time they jump, it will feel as if it takes ages to get up to the top of the water again. Add with a cheerful smile, the second jump will be much easier and

jumping into the deep end is really great fun. The children standing there, listening to you, don't believe a word you say; they are not happy at all and, if they had a chance, they would even run back to mummy. But the teacher should try to ignore the desperation on the little faces.

Pick the bravest one of the group and make him do it first. The others will be standing right at the water, looking down at the bubbles coming up from the child who has just jumped. A little head comes up to the top, grabs the ladder and says, 'Boy, that was good!' If a child is quite reluctant to go in, a little 'help' will be handy. Repeat the jumping about five times and that should do for their first deep water lesson.

One time in deep water doesn't qualify a child as fit to swim in deep water all the time. If a child can swim the width of an Olympic pool or twenty yards unaccompanied he can be left more to himself. If a child doesn't feel sure in himself, he will not play in deep water but rather stay in the shallow end of the pool.

If a child has been taught and shown how to jump in deep water, no great harm can come to him. Even if he is not confident enough to play in the deep, should he accidentally fall or be thrown in, he will know how to get up to the top of the water again, having experienced it before.

I know from personal experience that it's hard for a mother to believe that her child, who couldn't swim a stroke two or three weeks before, can now swim and play in deep water. My little girl, who was three at the time, simply refused to go near the deep end although by that time she was swimming—rather dog-paddling—in the shallow end. One day, some bigger girls (members of my husband Alex's swimming squad) took her into the deep end and made her jump in. From then on she never went back to the shallow part, saying, 'that was for babies only'. Some afternoons when the pool was filled with a capacity crowd, my heart would beat very fast when I saw her little head bobbing up and down among the other swimmers.

Kicking-board practice.
108, 109 'Boy, that's good.' Jumping into the big pool.

Teaching backstroke, butterfly, breaststroke.

ABOUT COMPETITIVE SWIMMING

There is a lot to be said for competitive swimming and, in the same breath, there is a lot to be said against.

How is a swimmer born?

A child learns to swim, does it without much effort and is usually entered into a swimming competition, e.g., in a school race; he wins it and from there on there is no way to stop him. He starts to spend more and more time at the swimming pool. Sooner or later he joins a swimming squad and a swimming club. At first he will train very light-heartedly, then he will get involved more and more, training twice a day. Swimming soon becomes a way of life.

Up until ten years ago, swimmers started competitive swimming around the age of 12 years and reached their peak at 18 or even as late as 22. This has changed dramatically with the introduction of age group swimming. There are competitions for under sevens, under eights, and so on. It is not unusual for a child, these days, to be in training *and* competition swimming at the age of six. Starting that early, they will often retire from swimming at the age of 14 years.

In my swimming days, it was thought that if a child started racing early he would burn out. This has been proven wrong. There is hardly such a thing as overtiring a child; at the age of six he is capable of doing six miles a day (in two training sessions), going to bed at night completely exhausted and waking in the morning ready to go again.

In my opinion, the very big advantage of competitive swimming is that children, very early in their lives, learn to be totally independent and learn that, if they want to achieve anything, they have to work for it themselves, and there is no mummy or daddy to help them. In a way this is cruel, but after all life is cruel too. A swimmer is a lonely person. Although the squad members are around, the swimmer has got to do the work entirely on his own. Unless there is a driving force behind

Butterfly arm stroke

him to do better and strive for perfection, he is never going to amount to much.

Swimmers have different motivations. Some do it for the pleasure of physical exhaustion, some to prove to themselves that they are capable of achieving something. Some will do it because of the pleasure of winning, some for health reasons and others, perhaps wrongly, will do it because mum said so.

There are many pleasures in training and competition and there are many disappointments, too. Losing an important race can become a tragedy. Social life suffers, there is no time for parties, visiting the zoo or even holidays. I must say, in fairness, that social life does exist but all your friends are fellow swimmers.

Starting at such an early age as six and subsequently retiring at an early age gives one the chance to catch up with other things.

From my personal experience I started competitive swimming at 11 years and stopped at 18½ years. After the Melbourne Olympic Games I had achieved everything I wanted—being a member of an Olympic team, travelling to many, many countries as a swimming representative, holding 20 or so national titles, leading the top ten in a world list in my particular event and the biggest of them all, being a member of a World Record Breaking Relay team—still, I often think if I was given another chance, would I do it again? Probably I would, but I often feel a social outcast for not being able to play tennis, ride a horse, ski, play the piano.

My fellow swimming coaches, including my husband, certainly disagree with me. They think becoming a champion is worth all sacrifices you have to make. I still think that competitive swimming is all right so long as nobody takes it too seriously. When families sacrifice so many years of their lives, giving up all their free time carting children to training sessions and swimming carnivals, I think it is a bit of a joke. Certainly there are a few exceptional talents and they should carry on by all means, but I see so many mediocre children involved in competitive swimming who really don't care one way or the other; their main motivation is that the parents get a big joy at

Jumping up and down in the water is so much fun.

seeing their offspring on the starting block. How often have I seen fathers scolding their children after a badly swum race? Competitive swimming should be between the coach and the pupil and *nobody else* should be involved.

The reader might ask why, after saying this, am I involved in the swimming game? Well, I love it! I love passing on my knowledge to children knowing that the gift I'm giving them will last a lifetime. Coaching is a bit like a lottery— occasionally one finds a perfectly talented, intelligent child, and to guide him until he achieves the top is a very satisfying achievement. Equally satisfying is to have a nervous, self-conscious child and through training and successful competitive swimming see him blossom into a self-assured, confident individual.

The swimming pool atmosphere is a very healthy one, with boys and girls mixing freely. Running around in swimming costumes, they don't look on each other as 'boy', 'girl', but rather as friends.

Schoolwork, surprisingly, doesn't suffer from all the outside school activities. Swimming children learn to concentrate much better than a non-swimmer would, so doing homework takes a half hour concentrated work compared with two hours for a non-swimmer who fidgets, plays and is distracted by TV.

BUTTERFLY STROKE
Standing out of the water, children should put both of their arms out straight in front of them and push them down to the legs. Keep pushing back as far as the arms go. At this point, the palms of the hands should be turned upward. With a roll of the shoulders, bring the arms over and around, so that they brush past the ears and arrive back at the original position. Repeat this a few times.

Back in the water say, 'Take a deep breath, face in the water and butterfly across the pool.'

One small voice, 'Kicking too?'

'No, Gregory, I purposely didn't say anything about kicking; do whatever you like.'

So the small group takes off. Two out of the four children

114

That's when you breathe in on butterfly
116, 117 Try to look like a butterfly.

will do natural dolphin kicking, one will drag his feet behind and move his arms only and one will do freestyle kicking with the butterfly arms. Keep repeating this and don't correct any of the kicking at all, just make sure that the arm stroke resembles the butterfly stroke.

Breathing

There are two ways of breathing for butterfly. One is to breathe every stroke (remember you always start counting a stroke in the front) and the other, to breathe on every second stroke.

When children are learning, it's easier for them to start off breathing on every second stroke and when they get stronger and more efficient they can revert back to breathing on every stroke.

Have the children hanging onto the edge of the pool and let them do some breathing and bubbling on the side, lifting their heads vertically.

'Try to take a quick breath and then try to blow out a very slow long bubble.'

First the teacher should demonstrate this, standing out of the pool. Arms stretched out in front, take a breath and bring the head down as if it is going into the water. Keep the head down for the completion of the first stroke, then, holding the head down still, make a complete circle again to finish the second stroke. This sounds highly technical, but in practice it's really easy.

Let the children practise this firstly standing in shoulder deep water, then walking along the pool. When the teacher is satisfied that all the children are breathing in at the beginning of the first stroke, she can then ask them to try to do it while they swim. Even at this stage there shouldn't be any correction or advice given on the kicking. This way even a four-year-old can butterfly ten, fifteen metres, doing the correct butterfly arm stroke and breathing without much effort.

Walking in pairs

To practise breathing and to make it easier, the children could do the following exercise.

Try to select children who are the same size and pair them off. The one in the front will lift both his legs up, stretch them

I am a snake, a rocking horse and a dolphin too.

out and hold them still. The other child behind grabs the legs
and holds onto them like a wheelbarrow, then starts walking
forward slowly and pushes the 'working-horse'. The 'working-
horse' starts butterflying, moving his arms and breathing.
At the end of the pool change around.

Doing butterfly this way is fun and the children seem to love
it. Walking in pairs could be used for breaststroke breathing, too.

Dolphin kicking

Have the children holding onto the edge of the pool, then ask
them to try to do a new kind of kicking—dolphin kicking.

Keeping the knees lightly together, move *both* of the legs
up and down vertically. The legs shouldn't be rigid, knees can
bend slightly and hips and the upper body can move as well.

'Does anybody know what a dolphin is?'

'It's a fish.'

'It's Flipper on television.'

'That's right. How about trying to be Flipper and try to swim
just like him?'

'But he doesn't do dolphin kicking.'

'Of course he does, he's a dolphin, silly.'

'Put your hands on the sides of your legs so you don't move
your arms, take a deep breath, face in the water and try to
dolphin kick across the pool. Look like a snake, like a rocking-
horse and a dolphin, all rolled into one. Don't be afraid to
wriggle your bottoms.'

So off they go. Surprisingly, they *all* do a perfect dolphin kick.

Have them practise dolphin kicking, first by holding their
hands on the side. Later on, the arms could be stretched out in
front. Practising dolphin kicking, holding onto a kicking-board,
makes them rather stiff, so try to avoid using the kicking-board.
When dolphin kicking goes fine put the arm movements and
dolphin kicking together.

I think I should digress to explain how that rather weird
thing of butterfly (insect) and dolphin (fish) came into being.

Once there were only three swimming strokes. Freestyle,
backstroke and breaststroke. At the 1952 Helsinki Olympics a
Hungarian girl won the 200 metres breaststroke event, using
butterfly arm strokes and breaststroke kicking in incredibly good

Backstroke land drill.

time. People using butterfly arm stroke in a breaststroke race were so much better than those who were doing ordinary breaststroke only, that the international swimming body decided to separate the two events. A little bit later on, some swimmers started to experiment with a new kind of kick to combine it with butterfly. The new kick resembled a dolphin's movements and that's how dolphin kicking was born.

The butterfly stroke has similar rules to those of breaststroke. Two hands have to touch the wall in a race, etc.

The general public thinks that butterfly is a hard stroke to do. It's not so. To do just a few strokes is very easy. To compete in a butterfly race is another matter. Without training and preparation it would be impossible. But the same goes for all strokes.

I found that children are very eager and willing to learn butterfly. Maybe it's the romantic name that appeals to them. In a few cases, I had children learning and swimming butterfly *before* they could do freestyle.

Anybody who is going to teach butterfly, please tell the children to watch where the wall is so they don't hit their head against the wall. Surprisingly, cut foreheads have occurred only when the children were doing butterfly. It somehow doesn't happen with any of the other strokes.

BACKSTROKE

Standing in the water, the children should move their arms first. Put one arm out in front so the thumb is facing upwards. Move the arm slowly up so that, by the time it reaches the ear, the palm of the hand should be turned outwards, and when the hand hits the water, the little finger should go into the water first.

Once under the water bring the hand down so that it touches the leg. When lifting it out again, be careful to bring it up very gently, so there is not much water dripping off. Practise one arm first, then the other and when everything goes well, start moving them both alternately.

Before the children start swimming backstroke, first have them walking backwards in the water, moving their arms.

Backstroke arm action.

Don't teach anybody to do backstroke arms unless they can do kicking on the back.

In backstroke, the body should be in a very flat position, the ears covered by the water and the kicking shouldn't be high. The above mentioned method for teaching backstroke is for beginners only. More advanced swimmers bend their arms under the water in an S-shape and the arm-pull usually finishes down 10 to 12 inches below the level of the hips. I only mentioned the bent arms so that, if a teacher sees a backstroker bending his arms, causing a little swell, he shouldn't correct it by saying, 'Keep your arms straight'.

The teacher with a good knowledge of swimming can teach children to push off on their backs from the wall, do an ordinary full-back turn, a racing start, and the daddy of them all, a backstroke tumble.

Since this book is not intended for describing advanced swimming techniques, we'll just leave it at that. There are excellent swimming books on the Australian market—one by Forbes Carlile and the other by Don Talbot—which have detailed illustrations and explanations of advanced swimming techniques.

BREASTSTROKE

'Has anyone seen a frog jumping or swimming? If you have, that's what breaststroke looks like.'

I have often heard that breaststroke is so easy, so graceful, so natural, and I say, to teach the correct breaststroke is absolute murder. It's ugly and very unnatural.

Breaststroke used to be pretty and graceful, until the Americans killed it. They analysed it, they photographed it, they dissected it and have cut out all the movements which were graceful and turned it into a power stroke. Actually, it was rather clever of them for, with the newly found breaststroke style, they chopped many seconds off the world records.

There is nothing much wrong with breaststroke, only the swimming rules are making it very difficult: arms and legs are not allowed to break the surface of the water; the head is not allowed to go under the water; everything has to be symmetrical;

125

Learning how to do backstroke push off.
126, 127   Feet turned out, heels facing each other . . .

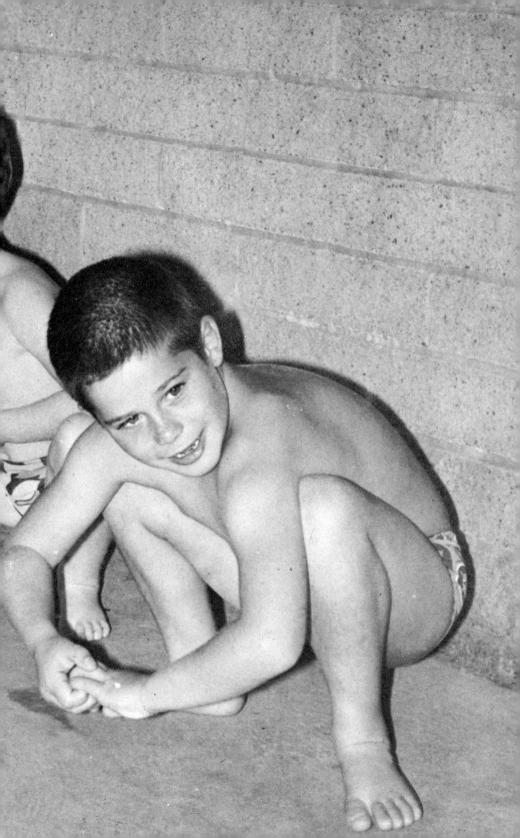

after diving in and turning, the swimmer is not allowed to do more than one stroke under water; at the touch of the wall both hands should touch on the water level. It's very easy to teach somebody breaststroke, i.e., a style which just resembles breaststroke, but it's very, very difficult to prepare a child for competition.

Before taking children into the water, they have to be shown how the breaststroke kick works. So, sitting on the floor, balancing on the backside, draw both knees up with heels facing each other and toes turned out, straighten the legs out, then bring them together.

Or have them standing, feet turned out, heels facing each other (a bit like first position in ballet). Squat down, turning knees out and keeping the heels firmly on the floor. While the children are squatting, explain that this is how you want them to hold their legs when they commence the kick.

Another exercise is to face and lean on the wall, draw one knee up with feet turned out sideways, then stretch the leg out backwards in a straight line without dropping out of the level, then draw back again to the original position. Repeating this about ten times, the children will feel the muscles in their thighs which are needed for doing breaststroke kicking.

In the water, have them practise breaststroke kicking, holding onto the side of the pool. Make sure that they don't drop a knee and keep both of their feet turned out.

'I want you to hold your arms out in front, don't move them, take a deep breath, hold it and try to breaststroke kick across the pool.'

After a few tries, with their feet only, they can try to move their arms as well.

Standing in shoulder-deep water, the arms are stretched out in front. Turn the back of the hands together (like an inside-out praying position), then gently pull sideways, about two inches under the water level. When arms are out fairly wide, bend them from the elbow, then gently bring the hands towards each other, then push out in front.

Breathing is similar to the butterfly stroke. You can breathe on every stroke or every second stroke. In the early learning

Mona Lisa and breaststroke kicking.

stages, I usually tell the children to breathe whenever they feel like it. Some of them will swim, holding their heads in, for about three or four strokes before they come up for air and some will come up every stroke.

In the advanced stage, swimmers come up for air every stroke and have a reasonably long glide at the end of the stroke. The head should come up for air when the arms are bending half-way through the stroke. The head stays down while the arms are going out to the front, glide, and pull back again to the bent elbow position. The breathing-in has to be very quick and the blowing-out very slow.

When children learn breaststroke, they have to spend many hours on the kicking-board practising the kick.

FREESTYLE

Freestyle swimming is the most popular stroke in Australia.

Australia has produced many great freestylers, e.g., Jon Henricks, Lorraine Crapp, Murray Rose, Dawn Fraser. We have produced other great swimming stars doing other strokes, e.g., Kevin Berry (butterfly), Ian O'Brien (breaststroke) and David Thiele (backstroke). These swimmers were equally great in their various swimming strokes and achievements but the general public takes more notice of the glamorous freestylers.

In all swimming competitions—school, state, national and Olympic—contestants compete in all four swimming strokes. Yet, not many teachers and swimming coaches are bothering to teach anything else but freestyle.

All learners should be taught all the strokes. By mastering all, they can specialise in the stroke which suits them best later on. When in training it breaks the monotony of the long miles to be able to switch from one stroke to the other. A freestyler, for instance, would gain great strength and stamina from doing a lot of work on the butterfly. Today, swimming coaches have their pupils do 75% of the work in freestyle and the rest is made up of other strokes. Towards main competition they swim more on their individual stroke.

In the early stages children were taught to swim with their arms straight. This way they were stretching out in front,

Breathing for breaststroke.
132, 133 Holding on to the wall for breaststroke kick

reaching deep down and recovering their arms at the very end of the stroke. The more advanced swimmers bring their arms forward slightly bent. The golden rule is that the elbow should be always higher than the rest of the arm. On entering the water the wrist should be firm, not stiff, and the arm should pull along the centre line of the body. When under the water, the arm doesn't pull down on a dead straight line but half-way through the stroke it bends as if the swimmer is writing a big S-shape with the hands.

When correcting a freestyle swimmer's stroke, stand in front of him and watch the entry and the pull from there. If the arm swings out to the side under the water, correct it immediately because it has to stay in the centre.

There are three types of breathing: breathing on every stroke, breathing on every three (bi-lateral) and breathing on every four. When the swimmer has to do some long slow swimming he could use breathing on every four. If the swimmer swims unevenly, rolls his body or doesn't lift one arm out as much as the other, he should do his training doing bi-lateral breathing. When racing a short distance, the swimmer needs a lot of oxygen, so in these cases he breathes on every stroke.

Breathing on every stroke
When the breathing arm comes out of the water, the head is turned back so that the swimmer may take a deep breath. As the breathing arm goes into the water, the head rolls down and starts blowing out. In that time the other arm makes a full circle.

Breathing on every third stroke (bi-lateral)
Put the right arm back, take a deep breath and as the right arm goes into the water start slowly blowing out. Keep the head in the water while the left arm makes a full circle and the right arm, too.

When the left arm comes out again, bring the head out of the water, turn to the left side, take a breath and put the head in when the left arm reaches into the water. Start blowing out and continue to breathe out for the next two strokes.

One—take a breath; two, three—face in the water. One—take a breath; two, three—face in the water.

134

This is how you pull under the water.

Breathing on every fourth stroke

Put the breathing arm back, take a big breath and blow it out slowly for the next three strokes. One—take a breath; two, three, four—blow out. One—take a breath; two, three, four—blow out.

In the beginning, children will stop many times, but as time goes on they will get stronger and stronger and so their distance will increase. If they are quite used to swimming in deep water, instruct them to do their training in the middle of the pool and not close to the wall.

The more advanced swimmers should learn how to push off from the wall. It's a relatively simple thing to do but it takes a lot of practice to do it properly. They have to learn to place both of their feet on the wall, push their head under the water before they kick off. Once they have learnt to push off properly they should learn to do turns and racing starts.

If training is carried out in an Olympic-size pool, the following programme could be carried out:

200 m. freestyle kicking on the board
200 m. one-arm breathing
200 m. freestyle
200 m. kicking on the back
200 m. backstroke
_____

1000 m.
_____

The following week, the freestyle and backstroke could be increased to 400 metres and by the end of the month to 800 metres.

Once children have learnt to swim fifteen or twenty yards there is nothing much left to do but to practise. The distance will slowly increase day by day. With proper guidance and swimming once a day, for a month, there is no reason why a child shouldn't be able to swim a mile by the end of a month.

The gift of swimming will last a lifetime. Remember, every great swimmer *once* had to be a beginner!

Never pull like this.

138, 139 *It looks good but it isn't. He is not breathing in and his eyes are closed.*

140 *Entering the water the wrist should be firm, and the arm should pull along the centre line of the baby.*